# MADEMOISELLE DE SCUDÉRY AND THE CARTE DE TENDRE

FM3

# Mademoiselle de Scudéry and the Carte de Tendre

## James S. Munro

UNIVERSITY OF DURHAM 1986

© James S. Munro 1986
ISBN 0 907310 12 5

# Contents

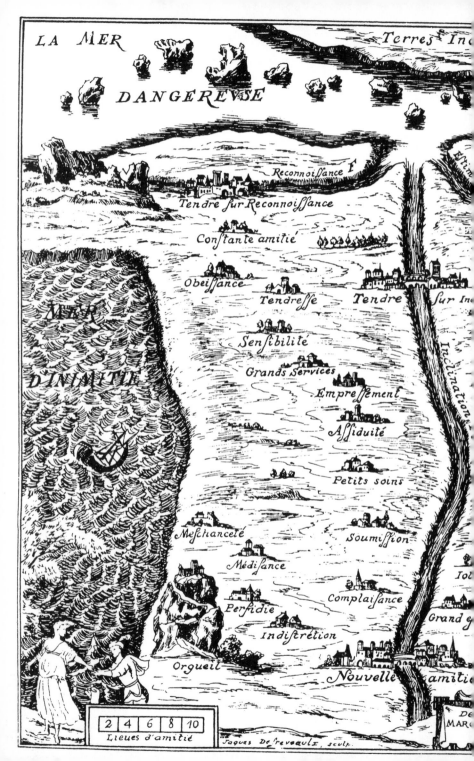

# INTRODUCTION

Of all Mlle de Scudéry's voluminous production, the part which is most widely known is undoubtedly the *Carte de Tendre*, the famous allegorical map which Mlle de Scudéry published in the first volume of her romance *Clélie* (1654). The *Carte de Tendre* is usually interpreted as a map of love, or more accurately of a rather suspect kind of *galanterie*; it has come to be looked on as a charter for the worst excesses of *préciosité*, for the mannered and rather cerebral courtship rituals satirized by Molière in *Les Précieuses ridicules*. Yet that is not how Mlle de Scudéry herself understood it, or intended others to understand it. When one begins to look at what the *Carte de Tendre* meant for its author, it very quickly becomes clear that the area of behaviour represented by the map cannot simply be equated with love; to continue Mlle de Scudéry's geographical figure, the *Pays de Tendre* is a different country from the *Royaume d'Amour*, although the two states have a common border. Still less can the *Carte de Tendre* be seen as an attempt to trivialize human relationships, to reduce them to the status of a society game in which the object of the participants is to seek their own gratification and amusement; to relationships of that kind, Mlle de Scudéry reacted with as much disapproval as the severest moralist. Indeed, it is one of the more savage ironies of literary history that the *Carte de Tendre* should so often be equated with a cold intellectualism, when for Mlle de Scudéry it stands for precisely the opposite - the investing of relationships with a new dignity through the rediscovery of genuine emotion.

9

The reading of the *Carte de Tendre* as a *carte d'amour* is one that goes back to Mlle de Scudéry's own time. There is in the seventeenth century a current of criticism which objects to the *Carte de Tendre* on moral grounds, seeing it as an encouragement to licence. In this perspective, the *amitié* with which the *Carte de Tendre* purports to be concerned is interpreted as a transparent fiction, an alias for love. Cotin, for example, slightingly refers to 'la Carte de Tendre, ou bien la Morale amoureuse, qui est le grand art de plaire aux Dames, si ingénieusement enseigné par vne pucelle'.[1] It is easy to dismiss this remark as the result of Cotin's own personal animosity to Mlle de Scudéry, occasioned by an epigram which he wrote on her deafness and which prompted a stinging reply made on her behalf by Ménage.[2] Personal animosity or not, however, Cotin's view is one which appears to have enjoyed some support. 'Desjà les Carmelites et les autres dévots et dévotes luy en veulent', writes Tallemant des Réaux of Mlle de Scudéry, 'parce qu'à leur goust c'est elle qui establit la galanterie, car les *Cartes de Tendre*, etc., et les Portraits ne viennent que de ses livres'.[3] Nor is such criticism confined to what one might call the religious establishment. In a work by Sorel entitled *Les Discours pour et contre l'amitié tendre*, there is a debate between representatives of opposing views, one defending *amitié tendre* and the other attacking it. 'En effet', laments the latter, 'combien pensons-nous qu'il se glisse d'abus sous le nom de cette belle amitié qu'on a inventée depuis peu?' To illustrate the point, a picture is painted of a man who sends a woman presents and letters, looks at her languishingly and speaks passionately; with heavy irony, the opponent of *amitié tendre* comments that 'ce n'est point Amour que ces Gens-là ressentent; Cela estoit bon autrefois: La Mode veut que ce soit maintenant Amitié'.[4] A more authoritative voice than Sorel's is of course that of Boileau, who in his *Dialogue des héros de roman* (1665) suggests that the *Carte de Tendre* is a map of the 'pays de galanterie' and that Clélie in Mlle de Scudéry's story draws up the map because she has 'pour Aronce une amitié qui tient de l'amour véritable'.[5] Such comments as these point to a marked reluctance on the part of Mlle de Scudéry's contemporaries to believe that the kind of relationship mapped by the *Carte de Tendre* can possibly be an innocent one; there is clearly an insistence, in some quarters at least, that *amitié* is to be glossed by *amour*.

Very much in the same vein is a much later attack by Boileau, containing what is perhaps the best known of all seventeenth-century references to the *Carte de Tendre*. This comes in Boileau's *Satire X*, and the fact that he should still be tilting at the *Carte de Tendre* nearly forty years after the latter's first appearance is an indication not only of the continuing popularity of Mlle de Scudéry's work but also of the lasting influence the *Carte de Tendre* may be said to have exercised on social attitudes. In his *Satire X*, Boileau talks of the various temptations which are likely to lead a woman astray; he pointedly remarks that if a wife's virtue survives the shock of Quinault's operas, it will inevitably succumb to a perusal of the *Carte de Tendre*. He then describes the process by which the married woman's faithfulness is destroyed:

> D'abord tu la verras, ainsi que dans Clélie,
> Recevant ses amans sous le doux nom d'amis,
> S'en tenir avec eux aux petits soins permis;
> Puis bientôt en grande eau sur le fleuve de Tendre
> Naviguer à souhait, tout dire et tout entendre,
> Et ne présume pas que Vénus, ou Satan,
> Souffre qu'elle en demeure aux termes du roman.[6]

It will be noted that Boileau's position here has shifted somewhat from the one he adopts in the *Dialogue des héros de roman*; *tendre amitié* is no longer simply dismissed as another name for love (by implication, the 'termes du roman' are chaste enough), but is now seen rather as the first step along the slippery slope leading to perdition. Support for this modified view of the *Carte de Tendre* comes from Arnauld, in a letter of Perrault prompted by the publication of Boileau's *Satire X*; like Boileau, Arnauld takes Mlle de Scudéry to task for 'la doucereuse morale qui s'enseigne au pays de Tendre', because, he believes, 'c'est par là qu'on va insensiblement au bord du précipice'.[7] Shift of ground or not, however, the basic thrust of these criticisms, made in the 1690s, is the same as that of judgments passed in the 1650s and 1660s: *tendre amitié* is called into question by being assimilated to love.

At first sight at least, it would seem that the verdict of such authoritative contemporaries (and the groundswell of opinion which they obviously represent) would lend powerful support to the traditional association of the *Carte de Tendre* with a particular kind of love. Yet it would be a mistake to give too much weight to the various remarks we have quoted. A recurring feature of these remarks is that they are mostly concerned not with what the *Carte de Tendre* was intended by Mlle de Scudéry to mean, but rather with the influence of the *Carte de Tendre* on social attitudes; in other words, their criticisms bear not so much on Mlle de Scudéry herself as on the use to which the *Carte de Tendre* was put in seventeenth-century *galanterie*. This distinction between original intention and actual use is of crucial importance in evaluating contemporary criticisms of the *Carte de Tendre*. It is certainly true that criticism of the *Carte de Tendre* is by no means incompatible with admiration of Mlle de Scudéry herself. Even in the *Dialogue des héros de roman*, which constitutes his most savage attack, Boileau writes that 'nonobstant la mauvaise morale enseignée dans ses romans', Mlle de Scudéry herself has 'encore plus de probité et d'honneur que d'esprit', adding that although the *Dialogue* was composed a long time previously (the middle of the 1660s, in fact) he had waited until after Mlle de Scudéry's death to publish it.[8] For his part, Arnauld too insists that he is not disputing the merit of 'la personne qui a composé la *Clélie*'.[9] Such a discrepancy between the judgment passed on the author and that passed on the work suggests that the concern of the critics is not primarily with the author's motive for creating; the problem is posed not by the literary work itself but by the impinging of that work on lived experience.

Evidence that the *Carte de Tendre* was quickly and lastingly appropriated into contemporary *galanterie* - in ways which Mlle de Scudéry herself would have repudiated - comes not only from Boileau and Arnauld but from other sources also. A sign of this appropriation is the penetration into the language of the vocabulary of the *Carte de Tendre* - items such as *tendre*, *tendresse*, *tendre amitié*. It is clear that with the publication of the *Carte de Tendre* such terms became hugely fashionable, part of the everyday currency of polite society. The influence of the *Carte de Tendre* on speech habits is rather curiously documented by a work of Sorel's entitled *Les Loix de la Galanterie*. Sorel first published this work in 1644, in a collection called *Nouveau Recueil des pièces les plus agréables de ce temps*. A second version of *Les Loix de la Galanterie*, updated and expanded in order to accommodate changes in social behaviour, appeared in the first volume of another collection, that known as the *Recueil de Sercy*, and published in 1659. Significantly, in the later version of the work Sorel adds a section of recommendations on how to speak, listing both useful expressions and expressions to be avoided; after reporting the current vogue of the word *furieusement*, Sorel adds that one of the things that should be said is 'qu'il y a du Tendre ou de la Tendresse en quelque chose'.[10] Initially at least, the terminology of the *Carte de Tendre* seems to have caused some surprise; on the expression *tendres amis*, Tallemant des Réaux comments 'Je doutte que ce soit trop bien parler'.[11] By the time Furetière published his dictionary in 1690, however, the use of *tendre* in such a context was evidently firmly established. Furetière begins by defining *tendre* in the clearly non-sexual context of *amitié* ('Il aime ses amis d'une amitié *tendre*'), but then adds 'on a raffiné en ce siecle sur les *tendres* amours', quoting specifically 'la carte du [*sic*] *Tendre* de Clélie'. The fact that *tendre* is commonly applied to love is made clear by further examples in which *tendre* is treated as a noun; expressions such as 'il a du *tendre* pour cette Dame' or 'elle a un furieux *tendre* pour ce cavalier' - in which *tendre* is being used simply as a synonym for *amour* - are obviously still current towards the end of the seventeenth century; as for *tendresse*, Furetière explicitly tells us that 'ce mot signifie le plus souvent *amour*'. It would appear from these quotations that the *Carte de Tendre* fathered upon society a new terminology which then continued to develop independently; Furetière is less concerned with the derivation of a word such as *tendre* than with the sense which it has come to have in the society which he observes.

The impact made by the *Carte de Tendre* on contemporary manners and speech is a striking example of a phenomenon which is characteristic of the seventeenth century as a whole, namely the high degree of interpenetration of literature and life. Like the literature of any other age, French literature of the seventeenth century of course reflects the society which gives it birth. In particular, the romances of Mlle de Scudéry constitute a very faithful representation of her own milieu, as is shown in the tendency, common since her own day, of seeking the originals of her fictional characters in the real-life people with whom she associated. *Le Grand Cyrus* and *Clélie* are both *romans à clef*, in each of which a different social group appears in transparent disguise - in *Cyrus* the *hôtel de Rambouillet*, in *Clélie* the guests at Mlle de Scudéry's own *samedis*. Yet the romances do not merely reflect a particular society, but also act upon society in their turn, catalysing changes in values and attitudes. Whatever else they may be, Mlle de Scudéry's romances are also manuals of good behaviour, prescriptive as well as descriptive, intended as a guide to living well in society. More important than their practical precepts, however, is the fact that the romances provide also a stock of ideals and goals; they represent not only society as it is, but society as it would like to be. Because of the spell they cast, the romances exercise a powerful pull on their readers to *vivre un roman*. Problems arise, however, when attempts are made to transpose the romance order of things into the less than perfect world of everyday experience; such is the tension between the ideal and the real that distortions and compromises must inevitably occur. The difficulties of adaptation are compounded when - as in Mlle de Scudéry's case - the ideas which originally reflect the thinking of a small select group are vulgarized and become common property, part of the intellectual baggage of an age.

This same distance between the original intentions behind the
*Carte de Tendre* and the use made of it in contemporary society is
a vital factor in evaluating not only the criticisms of Boileau
and Arnauld, but also the comments made on the *Carte de Tendre* by
an even more authoritative seventeenth-century voice, that of
Molière. It will be remembered that the *Carte de Tendre* is used
by Cathos and Magdelon, the heroines of *Les Précieuses ridicules*,
to justify their worst excesses. The two *précieuses* complain that
La Grange and Du Croisy are unacceptable as lovers because they
are unable to 'pousser le doux, le tendre et le passionné'; by
their bearing, they show 'qu'ils n'ont jamais vu la carte de
Tendre, et que Billets-Doux, Petits-Soins, Billets-Galants et
Jolis-Vers sont des terres inconnues pour eux' (Scene 4). Again,
the fact that the *précieuses ridicules* draw their inspiration from
the *Carte de Tendre* would seem, on the surface at least, to point
to a desire on Molière's part to ridicule Mlle de Scudéry. This
desire has in fact often been attributed to him, the protests he
makes in his preface (that he is attacking not 'les véritables
précieuses' but the 'mauvais singes qui les imitent mal') being
dismissed as a routine disclaimer designed to placate powerful
enemies. Molière's aim in *Les Précieuses ridicules* is a subject
of some debate, and the question cannot be aired in detail here.
It has recently been thoroughly investigated by Roger Lathuillère,
who argues persuasively that Molière's statement of intent in the
preface to the play must be taken seriously. The main arguments
which justify Lathuillère's conclusion are that the play was
performed in salons favourable to *préciosité*, and that Mlle de
Scudéry herself showed no enmity towards Molière - a striking
contrast with her attitude towards Boileau.[12] Like the moralists,
Molière is primarily interested not in literary history, but in
the social reality which he observes around him. What concerns
him is the behaviour of his contemporaries; to the extent that
Cathos and Magdelon can be said to represent current attitudes,
they are illustrations of the extent to which, five years after
its publication, the *Carte de Tendre* has become part of the
expected ritual of courtship.

The most telling argument in favour of the view that Molière is ridiculing not the *Carte de Tendre* but the use made of it comes however from Mlle de Scudéry herself. Even before the publication of the *Carte de Tendre*, it is clear that Mlle de Scudéry was plagued by inferior imitations of her style of life. In the last volume of *Le Grand Cyrus*, published in 1653, she introduces the character of Damophile, contrasting her unfavourably with 'Sapho' (the name under which she portrayed herself). Damophile models herself on Sapho, but because of her limitations succeeds only in appearing pedantic: 'Damophile ne disoit que de grands mots, qu'elle prononçoit d'un ton grave, & imperieux; quoy qu'elle ne dist que de petites choses: & Sapho au contraire ne se seruoit que de paroles ordinaires, pour en dire d'admirables'.[13] The original on whom Damophile was modelled has been variously identified: Alain Niderst suggests that she was Mme de Guedreville, whose portrait is given by Somaize under the name Galerice,[14] while Victor Cousin puts forward the name of Mme du Buisson.[15] The very fact that alternative suggestions can be made and argued indicates that imitation of Mlle de Scudéry was not an isolated phenomenon, and if that is true before the publication of the *Carte de Tendre* it is all the more so after. Like Mlle de Scudéry, like Molière in the preface to *Les Précieuses ridicules*, Sorel too provides evidence that a distinction was felt to exist, in some quarters at least, between genuine and imitation *préciosité*. In *Les Discours pour et contre l'amitié tendre*, Adraste, the opponent of *amitié tendre*, admits that not all *précieuses* can be dismissed as of no account: 'entre les Personnes qu'on nomme Precieuses, il s'en trouue assez pour qui ce nom ne doit point estre tourné en ridicule, & qui sont veritablement Precieuses & estimables'. The problem arises, he continues, because as well as *précieuses* of this admirable kind, there are also others: 'le mal s'est glissé imperceptiblement dans d'autres esprits depuis quelques années'. Works of fiction and poetry - even though they 'promettent seulement de monstrer l'effet de l'honneste amitié' - have nevertheless been misused and have given rise to 'nostre Amitié Tendre, qui est la cause de plusieurs désordres'.[16] As with the moral opprobrium of Boileau and Arnauld, so too with ridicule; it is necessary to discriminate between those who are its target and those who are not.

The authoritative seventeenth-century criticisms of the *Carte de Tendre* - those of Boileau, Arnauld and Molière - may thus be said to leave Mlle de Scudéry largely untouched, since they are principally concerned not with the ideas of Mlle de Scudéry herself, but with the *Carte de Tendre* as a contributory factor to *galanterie* and its effect on contemporary social life. Yet there has been a persistent tendency, even among critics who have made a special study of Mlle de Scudéry's work, to read these seventeenth-century judgments as if they represented the definitive verdict on the *Carte de Tendre*, and consequently to see the *Carte de Tendre* as a symbol of love more or less contaminated by *coquetterie*. According to the nineteenth-century critic E. Despois, the sentiment charted by the *Carte de Tendre* is no more than 'un amusement de société, une mode que doivent suivre les honnêtes gens', and consists of 'de molles et volontaires langueurs qui énervent l'âme et dépravent la volonté'.[17] A more recent writer, Dorothy Macdougall, refers to 'the delightful paths contrived in the *Carte de Tendre* by Madeleine de Scudéry for the excursions of her friends in the pastime of lovemaking'.[18] The latest of Mlle de Scudéry's biographers, Nicole Aronson, affirms that for many of Mlle de Scudéry's contemporaries, 'love was an intellectual occupation ... that helped them to fill the sentimental void in their lives', and that 'it is this sort of intellectual love that is described in the *Carte de Tendre*'.[19] Even when the charge of intellectualism is not explicitly made, it is still customary to interpret the *Carte de Tendre* as a *carte d'amour*. 'Tendre représente le sentiment Amour', writes E. Magne,[20] while P. Zumthor, the author of what is probably the most useful single article devoted specifically to the *Carte de Tendre*, declares just as categorically that 'les trois "Tendre" représentés sur la carte figurent trois états amoureux possibles'.[21] These statements constitute a valid description of what the *Carte de Tendre* came to mean in seventeenth-century society as a whole; at the same time, however, they present a very misleading picture of what it meant for Mlle de Scudéry and her immediate circle.

The purpose of the present study is to take a fresh look at the *Carte de Tendre* in accordance with what may be deduced of Mlle de Scudéry's original intentions. The task falls quite naturally into two parts. Before being incorporated into *Clélie*, the *Carte de Tendre* had already been in circulation as the product of the corporate life of the group which frequented Mlle de Scudéry; the circumstances surrounding the initial composition of the famous allegorical map must first of all be studied in order to see what light they throw on its meaning and significance. The composition of the *Carte de Tendre*, however, belongs not only to history but to fiction; by its insertion into *Clélie*, it becomes an event in an unfolding narrative, and at the same time part of a complex system of interrelated themes and ideas. Ironically perhaps, it is above all these themes and ideas which provide the stimulus for a revaluation of the meaning of the *Carte de Tendre*; the literary context provides an insight into lived experience, thus demonstrating yet another aspect of the seventeenth century's characteristic blurring of the dividing line between reality and fiction, the continuing dialectic between literature and life.

CHAPTER I

THE COMPOSITION OF THE *CARTE DE TENDRE*

1. *The Setting in Life*

The *Carte de Tendre* first came into being among the group of
friends which Mlle de Scudéry, from 1653 onwards, gathered round
her in the salon of her home in the rue de Beauce. Her favourite
day for receiving them was Saturday, hence the social gatherings
over which she presided came to be known as the *samedis*. The
*Carte de Tendre* however is not simply the distillation of the
spirit of the *samedis*; its immediate context is the personal
relationship which developed between Mlle de Scudéry and Paul
Pellisson soon after their initial meeting. The chief sources of
information both about the group spirit and about the personal
relationship are two documents emanating from the Scudéry milieu.
One is a manuscript known as the *Chronique du samedi*, which
preserves a number of letters and poems written by Mlle de Scudéry
and her closest associates. The manuscript itself is now
unfortunately lost, but extracts from it were published by L.
Belmont in 1902.[1] The other document is known as the *Gazette de
Tendre*, and this, like the *Chronique du samedi*, is a kind of
journal or minute book, recording the day-to-day happenings in the
life of Mlle de Scudéry and her friends. The *Gazette de Tendre*
forms part of a manuscript collection kept at the Bibliothèque de
l'Arsenal under the general title of the *Recueil Conrart*.
Extracts from the *Gazette de Tendre* were published both by E.
Colombey (1858)[2] and by E. de Barthélémy (1880).[3] Between them,
the *Chronique du samedi* and the *Gazette de Tendre* give valuable

19

insight into the social life of which Mlle de Scudéry was the centre. The *Chronique du samedi* (or at least the extracts from it published by Belmont) is chiefly concerned with the relationship between Mlle de Scudéry and Pellisson; the *Gazette de Tendre* adopts a rather wider focus, conveying something of the more general flavour of life in Mlle de Scudéry's circle. Both are of interest for the light they throw on the *Carte de Tendre*.

## 2. *The Relationship with Pellisson*

The first of the extracts from the *Chronique du samedi* reproduced by Belmont is a letter from Mlle de Scudéry to Pellisson, which demonstrates the privileged position which Pellisson had come to occupy at the time the letter was written; in it, Mlle de Scudéry confides to him the care of the letters and papers of which the *Chronique du samedi* is composed, thus making him a kind of minute secretary or archivist for her group. It is this letter which allows the composition of the *Carte de Tendre* to be dated with a fair degree of precision. Pellisson acknowledges receipt of the documents entrusted to him in a note dated 13 November 1653 (Belmont 652). At this point in the *Chronique du samedi*, there is according to Belmont a note which reads: 'Ici doit être la carte de Tendre qui fut faite ensuite au premier Samedi'. Misreading this last clause as 'qui fut faite ensuite *du* premier Samedi', Zumthor has suggested that the date of composition is either 8 November or 1 November; his reasoning appears to be (although he is not explicit about this) that the 'premier Samedi' must refer to the first Saturday of the month.[4] Pellisson's note, however, is quite unambiguous, and leaves no room for doubt that the *Carte de Tendre* was drawn up at the first Saturday meeting after 13 November 1653.

The relationship between Mlle de Scudéry and Pellisson had of course begun some time previously. The first significant event in that relationship was a journey to the country seat of Mme Arragonais at Romène, undertaken not only by Mlle de Scudéry and Pellisson, but also by Mme Boquet, Mlle Robineau, Conrart and Donneville (Belmont 656). Belmont gives the date of this journey as the summer of 1652, and in this he is followed by a more recent biographer of Mlle de Scudéry, Claude Aragonnès.[5] All the evidence of the correspondence which Belmont himself gives, however, points not to 1652 but to 1653; the letters concern themselves with events which obviously take place in 1653, such as the publication of Pellisson's *Histoire de l'Académie française* and subsequent reception into the Académie as a supernumerary member, and the publication of the last volume of *Le Grand Cyrus*, which appeared in September 1653. It would seem plausible to suppose that the *Carte de Tendre*, composed in November 1653, was the outgrowth of a relationship which had begun only a few months previously.

The main external influence on the growth of the relationship appears to have been Georges de Scudéry, Madeleine's brother, whose attitude was, in one sense at least, decisive. Taking umbrage at what had been said of him in the *Histoire de l'Académie française*, Georges de Scudéry forbade his sister to see Pellisson again (Belmont 662). Pained by the enforced separation, Pellisson wrote a letter to a mutual friend, Mme Boquet, who would, he knew, be certain to pass on any message to Mlle de Scudéry. In the letter, Pellisson describes his situation and his feelings by means of a transparent 'énigme', recounting his story as if it were a love affair: 'J'avais autrefois une maîtresse que j'aimais et que j'honorais beaucoup: mais depuis que l'injuste jalousie de ses parents me défendit de la voir chez elle, je vous jure que je l'aimai et que je l'honorai de la moitié davantage' (Belmont 662). In this scarcely veiled way, Pellisson affirms his intention to remain constant in the face of difficulties. Replying to this letter, Mlle de Scudéry takes the opportunity to establish a crucial distinction between *amitié* and *amour*, arguing that while resistance may increase the resolve of a lover, it is more likely to destroy that of a friend; in order to test whether this is true in Pellisson's case, she wishes to see whether after six months his determination will have altered in any way (Belmont 662f). Since Pellisson, in an editorial note, reveals that the trial period of six months was due to come to an end in February 1654

(Belmont 671), it follows that the 'énigme' letter and its reply must have been written in August 1653 and that the composition of the *Carte de Tendre*, in November 1653, must therefore have occurred about half way through the test of his constancy.

The precise circumstances surrounding the composition of the *Carte de Tendre* are given in some detail by Pellisson. In a note, he relates that the composition was inspired by a question from 'Acante' (Pellisson himself) to 'Sapho' (Mlle de Scudéry) concerning his standing with her:

> En une conversation du samedi, Sapho ayant fait sur le sujet de l'amitié une distinction entre ses nouveaux amis, ses particuliers amis et ses tendres amis, Acante demanda de quel rang il était, et on lui dit qu'il était des particuliers. Il s'avisa de demander s'il y avait bien loin de Particulier à Tendre, et si un homme qui marcherait toujours en diligence pourrait espérer d'y arriver depuis le mois de novembre où on était jusques au mois de février qui était celui où finissaient les six mois que Sapho avait pris pour l'éprouver. Il lui fut répondu que ce serait suivant la route qu'il tiendrait, parce que s'il manquait le chemin, il n'y arriverait jamais. Il demanda combien il y avait de routes: on lui dit qu'on y pouvait aller par eau, par terre et par air et qu'il choisirait laquelle des trois il voulait. Il dit que c'était la dernière comme la plus courte, et qu'il trouverait plutôt l'invention de voler. Sur quoi il fut parlé de plusieurs personnes qui avaient cru que cela n'était pas impossible ... Cette galanterie, au reste, étant poussée plus avant, donna naissance à la *Carte de Tendre* (Belmont 671).

It will be noted that the topography of *Tendre* as described here does not correspond with the version of the map published the following year in *Clélie*. Not only does the published version take as its starting point not *Particulier* but *Nouvelle-Amitié*; it also moves away from the initial idea of three different routes by air, by water, and by land, in favour of a scheme in which two routes are overland and one by water — a change perhaps prompted by the practical difficulties of differentiating between air and land routes on a map. What Pellisson is describing in his note is the germination of an idea, the process of creation which occurs when mind strikes against mind; his relationship with Mlle de Scudéry thus provides the context in which the *Carte de Tendre* must be set, and the immediate stimulus which led to its composition.

In February 1654, 'Acante' was notified by 'Sapho' that his period of probation had been successfully completed:

> Enfin, Acante, il faut se rendre,
> Votre esprit a charmé le mien.
> Je vous fais citoyen de Tendre,
> Mais, de grâce, n'en dites rien  (Belmont 673).

The question quite naturally arises of the nature of the intimacy to which Pellisson was admitted by this frequently quoted verse. Like the *Carte de Tendre* itself, the relationship from which it sprang is often presented as frivolous and superficial, a means of passing the time rather than a focus for genuine feeling. Belmont's own verdict is that 'nos amants se content fleurette l'un à l'autre; aujourd'hui ... nous dirions qu'ils flirtent' (650). According to Magne, the *Chronique du samedi* reveals Mlle de Scudéry to be an expert coquette against whose wiles the inexperienced Pellisson can only struggle in vain: 'La chronique montre comment, par ruses et par feintes, elle empaume le benêt, le transforme en "mourant", provoque sa déclaration, cherche, l'ayant obtenue, des occasions d'entrevues secrètes, témoigne tour à tour froideur ou amabilité passionnée'.[6] Other critics have qualified this view somewhat and have argued that although the relationship began as a flirtation, it developed subsequently into something more. G. Mongrédien, for example, echoes Magne when he finds in the *Chronique du samedi* manifestations of 'le jeu de la coquetterie, qui ne s'appelait pas encore le "flirt"'; at the same time, however, the mannerism and preciousness of the relationship is offset by echoes of 'une exquise sensibilité' in the correspondence, and by the gradual transformation of what had begun as a game into 'une véritable affaire de coeur'.[7] The position adopted by Mongrédien is similar to that of Macdougall, who talks of the 'judicious advances and retreats' by which 'the blue-stocking of forty-five was gradually to entice the enthusiastic young neophyte ... into her service'; as time goes by, however, Mlle de Scudéry and Pellisson see each other less and less as a simple amusement, and more and more because they have become necessary to each other.[8] Yet an examination of the *Chronique du samedi* suggests that these views may be less solidly based than they appear, and that they fail to do full justice to the kind of bond which is symbolized by the complex allegory of the *Carte de Tendre*. It is arguable that the relationship between Mlle de Scudéry and Pellisson is neither a flirtation nor an *affaire de coeur* but a kind of *affinité élective*; that, at least, is how Mlle de Scudéry herself appears to understand it.

It is of course true that there are certain features of the correspondence given in the *Chronique du samedi* which suggest that what exists between Mlle de Scudéry and Pellisson is to be defined as some kind of love. The chief of these features is that like love, the growing attachment documented by the *Chronique du samedi* generates jealousy. According to Belmont, there are in the *Chronique* a number of letters from Conrart, whose friendship with Mlle de Scudéry dates from before her encounter with Pellisson; in these letters, Conrart apparently expresses apprehension at the possibility of being ousted from her favour by the newcomer (Belmont 659). Unfortunately, Belmont gives the text of only one of these letters, written at a time when Conrart's jealousy was at its most intense and when Mlle de Scudéry was trying to appease him while simultaneously encouraging Pellisson (Belmont 671). Similarly, Mlle de Scudéry seems to have been jealous of Pellisson, who at the same time as seeking admission to the *royaume de Tendre* was engaged in the courtship of Geneviève Perricquet – a courtship which did not end until December 1653.[9] Certainly, Mlle de Scudéry did her best to terminate this courtship; there is a letter in which she insists that no person who is in love can be admitted 'au rang de mes plus tendres amis', because, as she explains, 'je fais consister toute la douceur de l'amitié à pouvoir penser que je fais la plus sensible félicité de. ceux à qui j'accorde la mienne' (Belmont 667). There is thus a desire for exclusiveness both in Conrart and in Mlle de Scudéry herself which seems to suggest that something more than ordinary friendship is involved. Moreover, Pellisson for his part has a tendency to speak of his relationship with Mlle de Scudéry in

24

terms of that of a lover with his mistress. This tendency is seen not only in the example, already quoted, of the 'énigme' letter sent to Mme Boquet, but also in a subsequent letter in which Pellisson expresses his deep disappointment at being kept waiting for entry into the intimate group of *tendres amis*: 'voulez-vous que je vous le dise, Mademoiselle! cela est insupportable; et l'amour, je dis l'amour en colère, avec toutes les flèches qu'on lui donne, n'a rien de plus terrible ni de plus fâcheux' (Belmont 667). Clearly, therefore, the least that can be said of the attachment is that it has affinities with love; the behaviour of the principal actors in the drama would not be noticeably different if Conrart and Pellisson were open rivals for Mlle de Scudéry's hand.

If the bond between Mlle de Scudéry and Pellisson is like love in some respects, however, there are also significant differences, and the evidence adduced above cannot be regarded as conclusive. Conrart may well exhibit jealousy, but at the same time it is strange that Pellisson should use him as a means of facilitating his own approach to Mlle de Scudéry and that he should request Conrart to transfer to him 'la moindre part de la part que vous avez en ses bonnes grâces' (Belmont 658). It is equally strange that Conrart, in the one letter of his from which Belmont quotes, should say of his attempt to maintain his position with Mlle de Scudéry, 'Mlle Conrart consent à tout ceci' (Belmont 672). Pellisson too expresses himself in similar terms, being sure that Geneviève Perricquet herself would consent to the place which Mlle de Scudéry occupies in his affections (Belmont 669). On the question of Pellisson's tendency to express his situation in terms of that of a lover and his mistress, it is noticeable that Mlle de Scudéry, in her reply to the 'énigme' letter, is careful to remove the possibility of confusion. It would have been easy for her to construe Pellisson's 'énigme' as a delicate declaration of love and to reply to it in kind; instead, she makes a clear distinction between *amitié* and *amour*, and it is in the name of the former, not the latter, that she imposes on Pellisson his six months of waiting. It is of course precisely this period of waiting which could be interpreted as *coquetterie*, the maintaining of the suitor's hope and interest while giving nothing. One wonders however whether *coquetterie* would not have been better served by admitting Pellisson to *tendre amitié* immediately, rather than making him wait. That is certainly the strategy of one contemporary coquette, the one described in Sorel's *Dialogue de la prude et de la coquette*; of her it is said that 'si quelque Amant se plaint d'elle, apres luy auoir donné quelques marques d'vne tendre amitié, à la premiere parole, elle le laisse plaindre tout seul'.[10]

Perhaps the most important factor which needs to be taken into account in assessing the nature of the relationship between Mlle de Scudéry and Pellisson is that *tendre amitié* has not only an individual dimension, but also a collective one. The *Chronique du samedi* makes it obvious that while Pellisson is seeking some kind of personal intimacy with Mlle de Scudéry, it is an intimacy which is not incompatible with the presence of other people; the question which it needs his period of probation to decide is essentially whether he is worthy of being admitted to a *group*, given a place in Mlle de Scudéry's small inner circle. More than once, Mlle de Scudéry speaks of whether Pellisson is to be received 'au rang de mes plus tendres amis' (Belmont 665, 667), and Pellisson's own account of the creation of the *Carte de Tendre* shows the conversation from which the *Carte* sprang to have been about the distinction made by Mlle de Scudéry between various groups, 'ses nouveaux amis, ses pariculiers amis et ses tendres amis' (Belmont 671). *Tendre amitié* may be exclusive, but at the same time it is relentlessly plural; the *Carte de Tendre* is designed to help Pellisson progress from one category to another. It is necessary because of the general difficulty, alluded to elsewhere in the *Chronique du samedi*, of knowing to which group one belongs: 'je n'ai presque point d'amies ni d'amis', writes Mlle de Scudéry, 'qui sachent positivement la place qu'ils occupent dans mon coeur'. The same letter stresses that while many are called, few are chosen: 'il y a un très petit nombre de personnes au monde, que je trouve dignes de toute la tendresse de mon amitié, quoiqu'il y en ait beaucoup que je trouve dignes de ma civilité, de mes louanges et de mon estime' (Belmont 669). Such remarks reveal that Mlle de Scudéry sees herself as surrounded by a series of concentric circles of friends of both sexes, and that as one progresses inwards each circle is more difficult of access than the last. Again, it is of course possible to construe such talk as a fiction, bait dangled before Pellisson to lure him on. However, the *Chronique du samedi* and more particularly the *Gazette de Tendre* show that such circles of friends do in fact exist; the Carte de Tendre is as much the manifesto of the spirit of Mlle de Scudéry's salon as it is a product of her individual friendship with Pellisson. To an examination of this collective dimension of the *Carte de Tendre* we must now turn.

## 3. *The Carte de Tendre and the Spirit of the Samedis*

It is clear from the contemporary documents that the group of Mlle de Scudéry's intimates was highly conscious of itself as a group and anxious to preserve its identity in the face of pressures from the outside. In this context, the *Carte de Tendre* appears as a kind of shibboleth, a rallying point for group loyalties; indeed, it was when Pellisson sought admission to the group that the *Carte de Tendre* was drawn up, codifying and institutionalizing procedures which may be assumed to have been already in existence. Once in circulation, the *Carte de Tendre* quickly became the centre of a wider set of allegorical relations. The group saw itself as citizens of the *pays de Tendre*, and the *Carte de Tendre* thus became a map of the group's 'homeland', a visible sign of its sense of unity. The *pays de Tendre* had its own archives, records of major events in the country's history, which have been preserved in the *Gazette de Tendre*. The *pays de Tendre* was organized, not unnaturally, along the lines of a monarchy, with 'Sapho', Mlle de Scudéry herself, as queen. In an initial period after the founding of *Tendre*, the monarchy appears to have been an absolute one; Sapho issued decrees in which she styled herself 'reine de Tendre, princesse d'Estime, dame de Reconnaissance, Inclination et terres adjacentes'.[11] As time went by, however,

the pressure of events brought about changes in the character of
the monarchy. A crisis occurred when some of the more notable
citizens of *Tendre* began to grumble over the way in which Sapho
was admitting newcomers. The *Gazette de Tendre* records the result
of this constitutional crisis in a document entitled *Relation de
ce qui s'est despuis peu passé à Tendre, avec le discours que fit
la souveraine de ce lieu aux habitants de l'Ancienne-Ville*.[12] An
account is given of a speech supposedly made by Sapho to her
subjects, in which she agreed to give up 'une partie de mon
authorité' and to constitute a 'conseil supreme' whose task would
be to scrutinize carefully any further applications to be admitted
to *Tendre*.[13] Thus Sapho, as Barthélémy puts it, 'transforma sa
royauté absolue en royauté constitutionnelle', restoring peace to
the kingdom.[14]

The question of the date of these events in the *pays de
Tendre* is an issue of some importance, for one of the newcomers
whose admission gave rise to the constitutional crisis was
Pellisson himself. According to Niderst, the various items of the
*Gazette de Tendre* 'datent visiblement du printemps et de l'été
1654', and when the citizens of *Tendre* were debating whether to
receive Pellisson into their number, Mlle de Scudéry 'l'avait déjà
reçu en secret'.[15] Niderst however gives no evidence for his date
of 1654, and it is arguable that the events in question could have
taken place earlier than he suggests. According to the *Gazette de
Tendre*, the citizens of *Tendre* objected to Pellisson's admission
on the grounds that before coming to the beginning of his journey
at *Nouvelle-Amitié* he had been exposed to a 'maladie contagieuse',
which is clearly love, since 'elle oste le repos; elle oste mesme
quelquefois la raison; elle fait tantost rire & tantost pleurer;
on soupire souvent, sans savoir pourquoy'. Consquently, Sapho was
asked to have Pellisson put 'en une maison destinée à la
purification de ceux qui ont esté en mauvais air'.[16] In other
words, the group's objection to Pellisson is his affair with
Geneviève Perricquet; it is the same objection as that raised by
Mlle de Scudéry, who, as we have seen, tries to terminate the
courtship, insisting to Pellisson that 'vous pouvez avoir de

l'amour sans être coupable, mais vous ne pouvez en avoir sans être un peu moins bien avec moi' (Belmont 667). In view of this similarity, it would seem plausible to suggest that the period of quarantine requested by the group need not be, as Niderst supposes, consecutive to the probation imposed on Pellisson by Mlle de Scudéry, but may be concurrent with it. If these two trial periods are in fact the same, the events recorded by the *Chronique du samedi* can be seen in a different light. It then becomes clear that the delay in admitting Pellisson to intimacy cannot simply be dismissed as the whims of a coquette blowing hot and cold; it expresses the intentions of the group as a whole; at the same time, Conrart's jealousy can be seen as the jealousy not of a lover but of a citizen of *Tendre* anxious to preserve his privileged position. Moreover, if it is indeed the group and not merely Mlle de Scudéry herself who kept Pellisson waiting until February 1654, then one particular detail of the rivalry between Conrart and Pellisson falls into place. We have already commented on the claim, made by both men, that their respective female partners back them in their bid for Mlle de Scudéry's good graces; this can only make sense if what is at stake is membership of the group (in which Mlle Conrart and Geneviève Perricquet can also participate) rather than an exclusive relationship with Mlle de Scudéry alone.

Whether Pellisson was subjected to one trial period or two, however, the fact remains that the *Carte de Tendre* cannot be properly understood unless its role as a group charter and manifesto is taken into consideration. From the *Gazette de Tendre* it emerges that Pellisson was not alone in seeking the route from *Nouvelle-Amitié* to *Tendre*. Indeed, part of the *Gazette de Tendre* consists of a series of reports from the various stopping places mentioned on the map, giving details of how different travellers are progressing with their journey. We are told for instance that Pellisson's whereabouts are not known, that Ysarn after reaching *Billet-doux* has become lost and is at *Oubly*, that Moreau has stopped at *Tiédeur*. Travelling in the *pays de Tendre*, however, is by no means an exclusively male preserve. The news of Mlle d'Arpajon is that she 's'est embarquée sur *le fleuve d'Inclination*', whereas the Comtesse de Rieux 'a pris le chemin de *Tendre-sur-Reconnaissance*'. As for the Duchesse de Saint-Simon, she has arrived at *Tendre* with unusual speed; having visited an island in the river of *Inclination* (an island which is not marked on the map), she found that the earth beneath her feet was moving, carrying her to *Tendre* almost at once.[17] The fact that both sexes are represented in the *pays de Tendre*, and in particular that two of the ladies mentioned travel to *Tendre* by the *Inclination* route, is a further indication that in the Scudéry circle at least, *tendresse* is not simply a definition of love; even the river of *Inclination*, fast flowing as it is, is not meant as an allegory of falling in love, and the presence on it of ladies who are also seeking to become Mlle de Scudéry's *tendres amies* suggests that it represents rather the immediate recognition of someone else as a kindred spirit, the awareness of a special affinity which, without making them lovers, may bind two people together.

To an even greater extent perhaps than the *Chronique du samedi*, the *Gazette de Tendre* demonstrates Mlle de Scudéry's anxiety to maintain the independence of her kingdom and to ward off any threat of encroachment from the neighbouring land of love. The decision that all new arrivals at *Nouvelle-Amitié* be carefully scrutinized seems to have been largely motivated by this desire to preserve the territorial integrity of the *pays de Tendre*. Of the reports given in the *Gazette de Tendre* from the various *étapes* shown on the map, the last - from *Tendre* itself - is the most significant in this respect. As has been pointed out, the objection which the citizens of *Tendre* levelled against Pellisson was that he had been exposed to the 'maladie contagieuse' of love; his quarantine is thus a measure designed to prevent the spread of infection. This same attempt to keep love out of the kingdom also lies behind objections raised to other candidates for admission, although it expresses itself in different ways. De Raincy, for example, is felt to be 'incapable de s'assujettir aux lois du païs'; in his case, the citizens of *Tendre* have decided 'qu'il avoit naturellement plus de penchant à l'amour qu'à l'amitié; et qu'il estoit enfin dangereux de le recevoir, si on ne vouloit exposer l'Estat à une révolution générale'. The verdict on Ysarn is perhaps even more instructive. His admission to *Tendre* is opposed first of all on the grounds that 'ses amours sont si tièdes, qu'il n'y a pas trop d'apparence qu'il soit capable d'une amitié ardente et tendre'; in other words, *tendre amitié* may not be the same as love, but the two are sufficiently close for performance in the one to be a good predictor of performance in the other. At the same time, however, doubts are cast on Ysarn's ability to renounce love, as he must do if he is to become a citizen of *Tendre*: 'il n'est même trop croyable, qu'il puisse s'empescher d'avoir toûjours quelque demy-maistresse; ce qui seroit d'un fort mauvais exemple dans *Tendre*, quand mesme on tomberoit d'accord que cela ne seroit pas dangereux'.[18] Behind these various allegorical devices - the risk of contagion, of revolution, of setting a bad example to the citizens - one may discern the group's fear of losing its identity, of changing its nature so much that it is no longer recognizable, of failing to prevent the *pays de Tendre* becoming simply another *pays d'amour*. The strength of this preoccupation shows the extent to which this threat must have been regarded as real.

If love disqualifies a lover from becoming a citizen of *Tendre*, or at least places obstacles in the way of his admission, the converse also holds, and any citizen of *Tendre* who wishes to become a lover must first receive special permission to leave the kingdom. The *Gazette de Tendre* preserves a document drawn up in the style of a royal decree, in which Ysarn is given permission by the monarch Sapho to absent himself temporarily in order to devote himself to *galanterie*. The decree is a special dispensation in Ysarn's favour, allowing him 'd'armer à ses despens un brigantin d'amour à voiles et à rames, mesme de faire construire, si la nécessité le requiert, une galère subtile pour éviter plus aisément les écueils de la Mer Dangereuse'. Ysarn is also to have the privilege of taking on board 'autant de munitions de guerre qu'il sera besoin pour l'expédition secrète qu'il entreprend, comme brûlots, grenades et autres feux d'artifice, dont on se sert

aux Terres inconnues, et qu'on appelle communément billets
amoureux, vers de galanterie, madrigaux et impromptus', and a
stock of 'stances, élégies, églogues et autres grosses pièces de
batterie, pour s'en servir seulement au cas où il seroit engagé au
siége de quelque place importante'.[19] The document is of interest
for the light it throws on the geography of the *pays de Tendre* and
its relationship with the land of love; the latter is represented
on the map by the *Terres Inconnues*, the tip of which can just be
seen across the rock-strewn *Mer Dangereuse*. In one sense,
therefore, the *pays d'Amour* is quite separate from the *pays de
Tendre*; Ysarn's absence is seen as a warlike raid on the coast of
an unfriendly country. Yet the equating of the *Terres Inconnues*
with the *pays d'Amour* means that the latter can also be seen as a
natural prolongation of the journey from *Nouvelle-Amitié* to
*Tendre*; after all, the three rivers shown on the *Carte de Tendre* -
*Inclination, Reconnaissance* and *Estime* - eventually join and flow
on into the *Mer Dangereuse*. The possibility remains open that a
man and a woman, having made the journey together from
*Nouvelle-Amitié* to *Tendre*, might decide not to stop there but to
travel on together, undertaking a more perilous voyage and
eventually disappearing into the uncharted interior of the *Terres
Inconnues*.

These relative positions of the *pays de Tendre* and the *pays
d'amour* are confirmed by another important document from the
*Gazette de Tendre*, providing not a map of the *pays de Tendre* but a
verbal description of it. This document, entitled *Discours
Geografique, Pour l'vtilité de ceux qui veulent apprendre la carte
pour aller de Particulier à Tendre*, may be, as Magne suggests, the
result of an initiative from Sapho's supreme council, composed of
Godeau, Conrart, Montausier and Chapelain.[20] It is also possible,
however, that the *Discours geografique* may be not an amplification
of the *Carte de Tendre* but a primitive version of it. The fact
that the starting point of the journey it describes is not
*Nouvelle-Amitié* but *Particulier* is more in accord with Pellisson's
account, in the *Chronique du samedi*, of how the *Carte de Tendre*
came into being (Belmont 671). Furthermore, the topography given

in the *Discours geografique* is slightly different from the published version of the *Carte de Tendre*. In the *Discours geografique*, all three routes to *Tendre* involve river journeys, and the traveller has a choice of a number of different ships in which he may embark; on the river *Estime* there are four ships (*Grand-Esprit*, *Iolis-vers*, *Billets-galants* and *Respects*), whereas on the river *Reconnaissance* there are six (*Complaisance*, *Sousmission*, *Obeïssance*, *Assiduité*, *Empressement* and *Petits Soins*). In the published version of the *Carte*, these names are of course given to *étapes*, which are much more numerous than the ships (ten on the road to *Tendre-sur-Reconnaissance*, eleven on the road to *Tendre-sur-Estime*); this may suggest that the *Discours geografique* represents an early draft which was later expanded. The possibility that the traveller will go astray is also more plausibly accounted for in the *Discours geografique* than in the published version of the *Carte*. In the river *Estime* there are three branching streams (*Oubly*, *Légéreté* and *Négligence*), each leading to the *Lac d'Indiférence*; the river *Reconnaissance* has only two (*Perfidie* and *Malignité*), both of which eventually flow into the *Mer d'Inimitié*. Once again, these names correspond to *étapes* in the published version, but are fewer in number. In the *Discours geografique*, there is no reference to the *Mer Dangereuse* and there appears to be no link made between the *Terres Inconnues* and love; we are merely told that 'les terres qui sont audelà des trois Tendre, entre toutes ces rivières, sont Inconnuës; lon croit que c'est vn païs si Infertile, qu'il n'y a point d'habitans'.[21] This relative imprecision also suggests that we are dealing with an early version of the *Carte*, and that the identification of the *Terres Inconnues* with the *pays d'amour* may have been a later addition.

Even though this identification is not explicitly made, the relative positions of the *pays de Tendre* and the *pays d'amour* – bordering each other, but independent states – are nevertheless confirmed by the *Discours geografique*. It is clear for instance that *tendre amitié* has something of the turbulence and uncertainty of a love relationship, and is thus a possible source of suffering as well as of happiness. Those who stray as far as the *Lac d'Indiférence*, we are told, 'sont des gens qui passent assez doucement leurs vies, qui n'ont pas de grands divertissemens, & dont les plaisirs sont simples, & Innocents; mais qui n'ont pas aussi de grandes Inquiétudes, & qui ne sont point sujets aux amertumes qui travaillent ceux de Tendre'. The contrast is obviously intended to emphasize the heightened experience enjoyed by travellers to *Tendre*, whose joys and sorrows, like those of a lover, are both exquisitely intense. At the same time, however, the *Discours geografique* underlines the importance of *tendre amitié* as the cohesive force which enables people in general to feel that they belong to the same group; it is as much a social as a personal manifestation. The description of the three towns of *Tendre* concentrates largely on how the inhabitants relate to one another and to newcomers. The inhabitants of *Tendre-sur-Inclination*, for example, 'sont extremement polis & courtois', receiving 'avec une bonté extraordinaire ceux qui abordent chez eux'; there is an absence of any satirical or critical spirit, and the town is 'le séjour des Eloges & des Panegyriques'. The citizens of *Tendre-sur-Estime* 'sont extremement civils, mais d'une civilité franche & qui n'est point importune', while those of *Tendre-sur-Reconnaissance* are 'Infiniment généreux'.[22] The various kinds of *tendresse* therefore have a common core of politeness and good manners; whatever else *tendre amitié* may signify, it is seen as a refined means of cementing social relationships.

The *Gazette de Tendre* may thus be said to show with particular clarity that the *Carte de Tendre* is not only the product of Mlle de Scudéry's fertile imagination, but that it belongs to a group; it reflects group thinking and at the same time provides an accepted framework within which group relationships can be understood and ordered. It is obvious therefore that *tendresse* cannot simply be equated with love. Yet *tendresse* is not totally unconnected with love either; the *pays de Tendre* and the *pays d'amour* may be different countries, but they are contiguous. In connection with this geographical situation, one further topic remains to be discussed. The *Carte de Tendre* is a social phenomenon not only in the sense that it affected contemporary *galanterie* and shaped the relationships of those most intimately associated with Mlle de Scudéry. A measure of the influence of the *Carte de Tendre* is that when it was published it gave rise to a host of imitations and claims to have provided the original which Mlle de Scudéry was alleged to have imitated. These imitations and claimed sources cannot be studied here in exhaustive detail, but some mention must be made of them for the light which they too shed on the interpretation of the *Carte de Tendre*.

### 4. *Sources and Imitations*

If an account of the circumstances surrounding the composition of the *Carte de Tendre* demonstrates the latter's collective dimension, what principally stands out from a study of the various imitations and claimed sources is the élite nature of the group whose ethos is summed up by the *Carte de Tendre*. At the risk of some over-simplification, it may be said that the *Carte de Tendre* represents an ideal to be striven for rather than a commonly observed reality, what should be rather than what is. The exclusiveness of the experience represented by the *Carte de Tendre* is already shown by the period of probation imposed on Pellisson, and by the fact that the map makes no attempt to disguise the pitfalls which await the traveller in the *pays de Tendre*; of those who seek the way to *Tendre*, not all will arrive. *Tendre amitié* is a kind of mystery into which the novice requires to be initiated, and it is above all this esoteric quality which is highlighted by a comparison with other contemporary allegories.

The didactic function of the *Carte de Tendre*, the obvious intention of showing the neophyte the way, links Mlle de Scudéry's map with a long tradition of allegories which have some kind of moral or spiritual basis. Such links were recognized in Mlle de Scudéry's own time. In 1653, shortly before the *Carte de Tendre* appeared in *Clélie*, Gilles Boileau published a work entitled *La Vie d'Epictete et l'Enchiridion ou l'Abbregé de sa Philosophie*,

*avec le tableau de Cébès*.  In a later edition of this work issued
in 1655, Boileau claims that the *tableau de Cébès* is 'l'original &
le modelle' on which other productions of this kind are based.  It
is clear that this claim is a response to the success of the *Carte
de Tendre*.  Boileau explains that he is not seeking in any way to
diminish the reputation which 'l'Illustre Mademoiselle de Scudéry
s'est acquise par sa belle & ingenieuse *Carte du Tendre*', adding
rather patronizingly: 'si ie ne lui donne pas la gloire de
l'inuention, au moins lui donné-ie celle d'auoir enchery sur
l'Original'.  The charge of plagiarism is not a very convincing
one, for the differences between the two works are more
immediately obvious than the similarities.  The *tableau de Cébès*
is not the map of an imaginary country, but the picture of a
castle that is meant to represent life; the castle, which unlike
the *Carte de Tendre* is peopled with allegorical characters,
contains three superimposed *enceintes*, the topmost standing for
what Boileau calls 'le *Siege* & la *Demeure* des *Bien heureux*'.[23]  The
journey thus prescribed by the *tableau de Cébès* thus takes place
on the vertical rather than on the horizontal plane, and concerns
not love specifically but abstractions such as goodness and
happiness; moreover, the world of the *tableau de Cébès* is a
totally enclosed one, with no opening towards the exterior.  While
the *tableau de Cébès* may have caused the idea of an allegorical
map to germinate in Mlle de Scudéry's mind, it would seem too
dissimilar to have served as an immediate source.

Modern critics too have set the *Carte de Tendre* against the
background of an allegorizing tradition comprising works of moral
seriousness.  Ernest H. Wilkins, for example, has suggested that
the immediate source of the *Carte de Tendre* was a map which, since
1525, had been included in editions of Petrarch.  This map was of
Vaucluse, Petrarch's place of enamourment; there are some general
resemblances between its topography and that of the *Carte de
Tendre* and, moreover, the Petrarchan map is concerned specifically
with love.[24]  Again, one may say that while such resemblances
undoubtedly exist, they do not seem sufficiently detailed to make
the plagiarism hypothesis a very plausible one.  Other critics

have pointed out affinities between the *Carte de Tendre* and works which are more explicitly spiritual in nature. Mongrédien points out that in 1650, Le Moyne had published an allegorical poem entitled *L'Isle de Pureté*, a description of an imaginary country 'où l'Amour Spirituel & innocent, est représenté par diuers Symboles'.[25] Zumthor has shown the *Carte de Tendre* to be related to 'une veine longtemps exploitée par les moralistes d'église', writers such as Guillaume de Digulleville, St John of the Cross and John Bunyan, whose *Pilgrim's Progress* appeared a number of years after the *Carte de Tendre* had been published.[26] Such works are not claimed as sources in the strict sense, but rather as representatives of a tradition to which the *Carte de Tendre* may be said to belong; as Magne has suggested, the publication of allegories in the years immediately preceding the *Carte de Tendre* provides not so much models to imitate as a ready made form which Mlle de Scudéry could fill with her own content.[27] On the *rapprochement* between the *Carte de Tendre* and this tradition of spiritual allegory, Zumthor writes: 'Je ne pense aucunement à une influence, encore que mainte précieuse soit classée par De Pure dans la catégorie des dévotes; je crois néanmoins digne de remarque cette identité de moyens d'expression, appliqués à des réalités dissemblables certes, mais analogues'.[28] In fact, the realities in question show an even greater degree of similarity than Zumthor admits; as we shall see, it is to a certain extent helpful to consider the *Carte de Tendre* as a transposition into the secular mode of ideas, common in religious circles, concerning different kinds of relationship between the believer and God.

If the *Carte de Tendre* may be said to have affinities with a tradition of spiritual allegory, it contrasts very markedly in this respect with the contemporary imitations to which it gave rise. Just as the *Carte de Tendre* cannot be said to be a slavish copy of the works which precede it, one may talk of 'imitations' only within certain limits. Derivatives of the *Carte de Tendre* do not go over the same ground, but set out to complement the *Carte de Tendre* by applying the principle of allegorical map making to new contexts. For the most part, they chart not the *pays de*

*Tendre* but the *pays d'amour*; there is a veritable spate of maps which are clearly designed to start where the *Carte de Tendre* leaves off and which provide a guide to travellers in the land of *galanterie*. In other words, they concern themselves with observed social behaviour, with what is rather than with what should be. The result is that often (though not invariably) they have a resonance which is lacking from the *Carte de Tendre*. The allegory becomes the vehicle for some kind of social comment, although it is not always clear precisely what that comment is (whether for instance it is meant as a criticism of the reality observed, or whether contemporary manners are being presented with a cynical wink of complicity towards the reader). It is noticeable too that, unlike the *Carte de Tendre*, which opens on to the *Terres Inconnues* and thus points beyond itself, maps of the *pays d'amour* (or more correctly, of the *pays de galanterie*), present an enclosed world, with no beyond. Such maps are therefore largely static, guides not so much to possible journeys as to notable features of the landscape which can, so to speak, be seen from where the reader stands. When journeys are described, they are frequently circular, bringing the traveller back to his point of departure. Unlike journeys in the *pays de Tendre*, those in the *pays de galanterie* do not lead anywhere, but simply give rise to endless repetitions of themselves.

In some cases, imitators of Mlle de Scudéry make no attempt to hide their indebtedness to the *Carte de Tendre*. One such imitator is Somaize, who in the fourth volume of the *Recueil de Sercy* (1661) published *La Grande Description de l'Estat Incarnadin, nouuellement découuert par le Lieutenant General du Royaume de la Galanterie*. The association with *galanterie*, already suggested by the title, is stressed by Somaize, who explains that his mythical state takes its name chiefly 'de l'inclination galante de ses Peuples, & du penchant qu'ils ont à aimer, l'Incarnadin estant la couleur de l'Amour'. Somaize quite unashamedly takes over Mlle de Scudéry's topography and applies it to his own *pays de galanterie*: 'Quatre Riuieres arrosent ce beau Païs ...; on les appelle, l'Inclination, la Reconnoissance, l'Estime, & le Tendre: les trois premieres se iettent en l'autre'.[29] That Somaize has in mind the impact of the *Carte de Tendre* on contemporary *galanterie* and is not on his own account equating *tendresse* and love is shown by another work of his in the same vein. This work, entitled *Le Voyageur fortuné dans les Indes du couchant, ov l'Amant heureux*, had already appeared in an earlier volume of the *Recueil de Sercy*. Again the debt to Mlle de Scudéry is quite specific; the work's title page announces that it contains 'la découuerte des Terres inconnuës qui sont au delà des trois Villes de Tendre'. According to Somaize, the objective of the traveller who arrives in the *Terres Inconnues* is to arrive at *Joüissance*; starting from the river of *Doux-Regard*, one may progress either by the short route through *Temerité* (a difficult road to take 'à cause des precipices'), or alternatively reach *Joüissance* by way of *Privautez*, *Baiser*, *Embrassement* and *Attouchement*. The fruits which are eaten at *Joüissance* give the lover a stomach complaint called 'la maladie de *Dégoust*'; the remedy is to go and take the waters at *Nouueauté*, near to the point at which the river of *Doux-Regard* flows into the *Mer Dangereuse*. It is thus a typical circular itinerary in the domain of sexual conquest, a domain which Somaize recognizes to be independent of that represented by the *Carte de Tendre*; he points out to the inhabitants of *Tendre* 'la faute qu'ils font de negliger la conqueste d'vn si riche Pays'.[30] The explicitly sexual character of the relationships which according to Somaize are symbolized by the *Terres Inconnues* throws into greater relief what he understands to be the essentially non-sexual nature of *tendresse*.

In addition to Somaize's two supplements to the *Carte de Tendre*, the *Recueil de Sercy* contains a further attempt to fill in the missing details of the *Terres Inconnues*. This takes the form of a *Lettre de M.D. sur la Carte du Royaume de Tendre écrite à l'illustre M.S.*, the latter set of initials being of course those of Madeleine de Scudéry herself. Again the *Terres Inconnues* are seen as the land inhabited by *galanterie*; the only commerce allowed is in human hearts. There are those who try to obtain the heart of another by languishing and sighing for years at a time; such old-fashioned constant lovers, however, are no match for 'certains blondins', with their fans, their lace, their precious stones and perfumes. The best way to reach the *Terres Inconnues* is by a little path which the *Carte de Tendre* fails to mention: 'on l'appelle le sentier du Hazard; on passe pour y arriuer, par vn Bois qui se nomme des Bonnes Fortunes, & il se termine à vn Pont qu'on appelle Foiblesse feminine'. Although perhaps less explicit that Somaize's *Voyageur fortuné*, the *Lettre de M.D.* clearly charts a similar realm of experience. Like Somaize, the author of the *Lettre* is at pains to stress that this realm is not to be confused with that of *Tendre*, insisting that the hearts exchanged in the *Terres Inconnues* 'sont d'vn vsage plus commode que ceux de la Ville de Tendre; car ceux de cette Ville de Tendre sont gardez dans vn Magasin public, dont la Concierge est vne ancienne Dame nommée Grande Vertu, qui n'en permet l'entrée qu'à fort peu de gens. Elle demande des certificats de Longue Connoissance, des attestations de Bel Esprit, & des passeports de Bonne Reputation'.[31] This emphasis on the relative difficulty of relationships in the *pays de Tendre* is a further reminder that *tendresse* is open only to a select few; far from being the same as *galanterie*, it represents a reaction to it, an attempt to rise above what is felt as commonplace and everyday.

Like the tradition of spiritual allegory from which Mlle de Scudéry may have drawn some of her inspiration, the convention that seeks to chart the topography of the *pays de galanterie* appears to be anterior to the creation of the *Carte de Tendre* itself, providing not only derivatives such as those mentioned above, but also a number of possible sources. One such possible is a work entitled *La Carte du Royaume d'Amour ou la description succinte de la contrée qu'il régit, de ses principales Villes, Bourgades & autres lieux, & le chemin qu'il faut tenir pour y faire voyage*. This *Carte du Royaume d'Amour* appeared in 1659 in the first volume of the *Recueil de Sercy*, where it is attributed to Tristan l'Hermite. As Zumthor remarks, if the attribution is correct, the *Carte du Royaume d'Amour* must have been composed in

1653-4, the period immediately preceding Tristan's death;[32] it is thus almost exactly contemporary with the *Carte de Tendre*, and may even pre-date it. Again, however, the differences between the two imaginary countries are more apparent than the similarities. As is the case in Somaize's *Voyageur fortuné*, the destination for Tristan's pilgrim is *Joüissance*. The allegory transparently represents the development of a particular kind of liaison which must have been commonplace at the time; having met in the wood called *Belle-Assemblée*, 'qui est vn bois fort agreable où il y a presque tousiours Concerts de Luths & de Voix, ou du moins la grande Bande des Violons & souuent la Comedie & le Bal', the lovers pass through *Reueuë*, *Visite* and *Soûpirs* to a town known as *Soins-sur-Complaisance*, notable for its university in which the staff are 'passez Docteurs en Fleurettes, Rondeaux, Bouts-Rimez, Triolets, Bons mots, & Contes agreables'. From here, *Joüissance* is reached by way of *Feu déclaré*, *Protestations* and *Entreprendre*, where, we are told, 'il y auoit autrefois ... vn chasteau mediocrement fortifié, qu'on appelloit Resistance; mais il a esté ruiné par les guerres, & de son débris on a fait vne petite bicoque qu'on nomme Tost-renduë'. Beyond *Joüissance* there lie *Satieté* and *Faible Amitié*, the latter being 'tout contre Inclination nouuelle, ioignant Doux-Regard, dans le Bois de Belle Assemblée; tellement qu'il semble qu'on n'ait fait qu'vn circuit dans toute la Region d'Amour'.[33] Here too the similarity with Somaize is striking; the journeys described by the *Carte du Royaume d'Amour* and by the *Voyageur fortuné* end where they began, and thus never end at all. The traveller has no choice; if he wishes to travel at all, he is condemned to go round and round on the same route, and this weight of inevitability suggests that Tristan's aim, like that of Somaize, is to record experience rather than to seek to change it. Whether Tristan is to be considered a predecessor or a successor of Mlle de Scudéry, he is clearly not attempting to describe the same country.

Another author with some claim to have been a precursor of Mlle de Scudéry in the art of allegorical map-making is the Abbé d'Aubignac, whose *Nouvelle Histoire du temps ou Relation véritable*

*du Royaume de Coquetterie* appeared in 1654. From a later edition
of this work, published in 1659, it appears that d'Aubignac was
accused of having plagiarized the *Carte de Tendre*, for in a
prefatory letter he is pains to defend his own originality. He
asserts that his own description of the *Royaume de Coquetterie* was
compiled before the *Carte de Tendre* and that, when the latter
production was shown to him by Mlle de Scudéry, 'ie luy dis que
i'auois dés long-temps fait vne description de la vie des femmes
extrauagantes que l'on nomme Coquettes, mais que ma profession
presente m'empesche de faire voir de quel air ie les auois
traitées'. Such a claim is of course difficult to prove, and, as
if conscious of this, d'Aubignac reinforces his defence against
the charge of plagiarism with a more convincing argument. He
points out the essential differences between the *Royaume de
Coquetterie* and the *Carte de Tendre*, insisting that *coquetterie*
must be considered to have existed before *tendre amitié* appeared
on the scene: 'Non, non, la Coqueterie n'est point la fille de
*Tendre*, elle est bien plus âgée que luy, elle n'a pas grand
commerce dans ce pays, & quand elle y fait voyage, elle court
fortune de se perdre'. This difference in intention, he
continues, is reflected in a difference in topography; whereas in
the *pays de Tendre* villages are very near each other, so that 'les
voyageurs n'ont pas seulement le loisir de se lasser', in the
*Royaume de Coquetterie* 'les chemins ne sont point remplis de tant
de gistes; c'est vn pays où l'on doit aller viste, & faire de
longues traites si l'on veut arriuer à ses fins'.[34] The
distinction made by d'Aubignac is amply confirmed by the map of
the *Royaume de Coquetterie* itself. This again is a closed,
self-contained world, being in the form of an ellipse, with no
opening towards the exterior. Its main feature is a number of
alternative routes by which one may travel from the capital of the
kingdom to the *Palais des Bonnes-Fortunes*, where the sovereign of
the country, a prince called *Amour-coquet*, holds court; these
routes include the *route d'Or*, the *gué de l'Occasion*, the *fort de
l'Entreprise*, and the *montagnes des Avances*. Outside this central
region, there are other interesting places for the tourist to

visit, including a *Place de Cajolerie* and an enclosed arena set apart for the *combat des belles jupes*. These names, like Tristan's *Bois de Belle-Assemblée*, evoke the fashionable meeting places in which the polite society of the time was accustomed to assemble, and which thus offered numerous possibilities for amorous adventures.

Of all contemporary allegories, it is the *Royaume de Coquetterie* which is most explicitly aware of the differences between the *pays de Tendre* and the *pays de galanterie*, and which perhaps gives the most detailed and revealing description of the latter. D'Aubignac spends a considerable amount of time classifying and cataloguing the inhabitants of the *Royaume de Coquetterie*, and the names he gives to the various classes provide an insight into the kind of behaviour which he considers to be within the province of *Amour-coquet*. Males he divides into 'les soupirans, qui ne sont jamais vêtus que de chagrin de couleur de pensée à fond de souci', 'les aventuriers, 'les ânes d'or', and 'les Coeurs-volans', this last being a sect founded by the inconstant Hilas, with, as its motto, the phrase 'qui plus en aime, plus aime'. Women fall into categories such as 'les Admirables', 'les Précieuses, qui maintenant se donnent à bon marché', 'Ravissantes', 'Mignones', 'Evaporées', 'Embarrassées', and 'Barbouillées'. There are also what d'Aubignac calls 'les Mal-assorties', that is, those who, 'condamnées injustement à souffrir la domination d'un vieillard, d'un fâcheux ou d'un sot ... se sont pourvues au conseil de l'Amour-coquet'. The inhabitants of the country are strongly influenced by allegorical characters such as *l'Intrigue* and *la Mode*; of the latter it is said that she exercises 'l'intendance des étoffes, couleurs & façons'. References are made to 'académies' which represent the salons of the time, to the importance of gambling, and to some of the extravagances of a luxury-loving society; in the capital city there is a shop full of 'fers à friser de toutes figures, boëtes à mouches d'or & d'argent, poudres de senteurs, miroirs, masques, rubans, éventails, papier doré, brasselets de cheveux, peignes de poche, relève-moustaches, bijoux, essences, opiates, gommes, pommades, & autres ustensiles de ménage'. As for the ruler of the country, Prince *Amour-coquet*, he is said to be a brother of *Amour*, 'mais frère bâtard, enfant de la Nature, & du Désordre', the result being that 'ses affaires sont plus mêlées d'intérêt que d'affection, & les déréglemens de la débauche y sont plus approuvés que la conduite de la Raison'.[35] D'Aubignac is not simply reporting what he claims to see around him, but judging it. He adopts a critical attitude to the displacement of affection by self-interest, and in this at least, as we shall see, he and Mlle de Scudéry speak with one voice.

Whether or not Tristan's *Carte du Royaume d'Amour* and d'Aubignac's *Royaume de Coquetterie* were composed before or after the *Carte de Tendre*, the fact remains that, together with the various derivatives mentioned above, they point to the existence, in the society of Mlle de Scudéry's time, of a particular tradition of *galanterie* within which relationships between the sexes are typically acted out. *Galanterie* is characterized by its superficiality and transience, by caprice and whim and changing fashion, by its strong association with money and material luxuries, above all perhaps by self-interest, by a quest for self-gratification and pleasure in its various forms, including of course sexual pleasure; in the *pays de galanterie*, the chief aim is to reach *Jouïssance*. It is precisely *galanterie*, in other words, which reduces love to a game, played according to generally accepted rules and conventions. Yet comparison with maps of the *pays de galanterie* shows that however much the *Carte de Tendre* may later have been incorporated into the game, it was originally felt to have nothing to do with *galanterie* and to concern itself with quite a different area of experience. Like the spiritual allegories with which it has been associated, the *Carte de Tendre* represents the quest for a higher reality. Its difficult itinerary is designed to take people from where they are and to point them beyond; the traveller who reaches *Tendre* from *Nouvelle-Amitié* has not only moved but progressed, been enlightened and initiated into a richer realm of existence.

It may be said then that a study of the circumstances surrounding the composition of the *Carte de Tendre* is of interest chiefly for the degree of precision with which (to continue Mlle de Scudéry's own metaphor) it allows the geographical situation of the *pays de Tendre* to be defined. The *pays de Tendre* lies close to the land of love, since from an early stage the latter is identified with the *Terres Inconnues*; at the same time, however, the two countries are not the same. In particular, as other contemporary allegories show, the *pays de Tendre* is very different from the *pays de galanterie* which, authors claim, represents the society they see around them; *tendresse* is a force which not only unites a man and a woman, but provides a focus for a group, small and select though that group may be. The history of how the *Carte de Tendre* came into being and how it was received cannot, however, reveal the objective reality behind the allegorizing, and to find this one must consider the *Carte de Tendre* as a literary device, its place in *Clélie* and in the wider context of Mlle de Scudéry's global vision. The real life experience of *tendresse* is constantly expressed, by Mlle de Scudéry and her group, in the coded language of allegory; conversely, it is the metaphorical world of fiction which allows the real-life experience to be rendered in plain language.

CHAPTER II

THE *CARTE DE TENDRE* AS A LITERARY DEVICE

1. *The Setting in Literature*

According to Tallemant des Réaux, it was Chapelain who suggested
that the *Carte de Tendre* be incorporated into *Clélie*.[1] Mlle de
Scudéry readily complied. The *Carte de Tendre* duly appeared in
volume I of *Clélie* which - since it was published along with
volume II in August 1654 - must have been composed earlier in the
year, perhaps around the time when Pellisson's period of probation
was coming to an end. The decision to include the *Carte de Tendre*
in *Clélie* is a clear indication that from the outset the new
romance is conceived as mirroring the life of Mlle de Scudéry's
circle; for all its setting in ancient Rome, *Clélie* has its roots
in the *pays de Tendre*. In the romance, the making of the *Carte de
Tendre* is a significant event in the plot, belonging to the early
stages of the unfolding relationship between the two principal
characters, Aronce and Clélie. The sequence of events which in
the fictional narrative leads up to the composition of the *Carte
de Tendre* is clearly modelled on the historical events which
actually took place among Mlle de Scudéry's friends; for all the
inevitable idealization and distortion, therefore, the version of
events given in *Clélie* is an indication of how Mlle de Scudéry
herself interprets the *Carte de Tendre* and wishes others to
interpret it. At the same time, however, it is not only this
incorporation into the plot of *Clélie* which acts as a commentary
on the *Carte de Tendre*. The romance records not only events but
discussions, not only something of the history of the *samedis*

46

group but also its preoccupations, its favourite topics of
conversation and characteristic responses to the questions it
raises. Seen against this background, the *Carte de Tendre* appears
not as a frivolous game but as a kind of convenient shorthand
representation of a whole view of human relationships, a
distillation of the spirit of Mlle de Scudéry's circle as well as
a record of a particular event in its history.

## 2. *The Composition of the Carte de Tendre as described in Clélie*

The circumstances which, in the fictional world of *Clélie*, give
rise to the composition of the *Carte de Tendre* are described by a
friend of Aronce named Celere, who early in volume I recounts the
'Histoire d'Aronce et de Clélie' (I, 89ff).[2] Celere's story falls
naturally into two stages, one set in Carthage, the other in
Capua. The first of these two stages is concerned very largely
with the early life of the principal characters in the story.
Aronce, it transpires, is in reality the son of King Porsenna, but
for political reasons has had to be separated from his parents
while still a baby. The parents of Clélie, Clelius and Sulpicie,
have adopted the baby Aronce and named him in memory of a dead son
of their own. The family settle in Carthage. Here Aronce becomes
friendly with the Prince of Carthage and with a nobleman called
Amilcar. With his two friends, Aronce, now sixteen years of age,
journeys to Greece and Rome; when they return, four years later,
Aronce is twenty and Clélie sixteen. In Rome they have met Horace
– none other than the Horatius Cocles, who will later hold single-
handed the bridge over the River Tiber – and Horace returns with
them to Carthage. Clélie has by this time become extraordinarily
beautiful, and has a number of high-ranking suitors, though it is
emphasized that as yet she herself has no experience of love: 'le
coeur de cette admirable Fille, estoit encore vn coeur où personne
n'auoit de part' (I, 171). Predictably, both Horace and Aronce
fall in love with Clélie, although they do not yet realize that
they are rivals. At this point, the tone changes; the highly
romanesque sequence of events is interrupted by the lengthy
account of a conversation in which all the chief characters

participate. The members of the group begin by debating whether love depends on knowing the beloved well, and then turn their attention to the nature of *tendresse* - a crucial discussion which we shall analyse in some detail later. After this gathering, there follows a period of separation for Aronce and Clélie. In an attempt to conquer his love, Aronce goes off to war, and after his departure Clélie and her parents are forced to leave Carthage in order to escape the unwelcome attentions of one of her suitors. Setting off to look for Clélie, Aronce encounters a pirate ship, which he attacks and overcomes; on board, he finds Clélie and her family, together with Horace. The company arrives in Capua, and decides to settle there.

In the part of the story set in Capua, there is the same rather strange combination of highly romanesque events and discussions which give the impression of having been drawn from life. Clélie's beauty makes her the talk of Capua and she soon finds herself at the centre of the town's social life. Celere reports debates on whether Clélie would be more beautiful if she deliberately set out to be so (I, 303ff), and on why 'la plus part des Belles sont auares de louanges' (I, 322ff). As far as the relationship between Aronce and Clélie is concerned, the main development which occurs in Capua is the increasing rivalry of Aronce and Horace. Almost simultaneously they write letters to Clélie in which they declare their love; Clélie, receiving the two letters at the same time, suspects that she is the victim of a practical joke, a suspicion confirmed when both rivals arrive together to see her. The coincidence makes Aronce and Horace realize for the first time that they are rivals; they discuss their situation, and promise 'de ne s'entre-nuire point aupres de Clélie' (I, 384). Each adopts a different strategy with Clélie. Horace decides 'de la presser continuellement de luy vouloir estre fauorable', whereas Aronce resolves 'qu'il ne demanderoit autre chose que la seule grace d'estre creû son Amant, quoy qu'il ne pretendist d'en estre aimé, que comme le premier d'un petit nombre de Gens que Clélie apelloit ses tendres Amis' (I, 385). In other words, Aronce sets his sights lower than Horace; unwilling to seek

to be loved by Clélie (because to do so would be to make demands
of her which would be inconsistent with his respect for her and
with his conviction of his own unworthiness), he will accept
*tendre amitié* as an adequate return for his love of her. Although
Aronce's strategy is dictated not by a calculation of its likely
results but by the kind of person he is, his choice turns out to
be a happy one, for he progresses more quickly than Horace in
Clélie's affections. In affairs of the heart, it would seem, the
best way to hold on is to let go, or at least not to grasp too
tightly.

This allusion by Aronce to Clélie's *tendres amis* prepares the
way for the introduction into the story of the episode which
describes how the *Carte de Tendre* was composed. What precipitates
the composition is the arrival of a newcomer from Rome called
Herminius, who is, we are told, as anxious to gain Clélie's
friendship as her suitors are to gain her love. It is to
Herminius that Clélie describes the different categories into
which she, like Mlle de Scudéry herself, divides her friends:

> Il ne faut pas conclurre ... que tous ceux que i'appelle mes
> Amis, soient de mes tendres Amis, car i'en ay de toutes les
> façons dont on en peut auoir. En effet i'ay de ces demis
> Amis, s'il est permis de parler ainsi, qu'on apelle autrement
> d'agreables connoissances: i'en ay qui sont vn peu plus
> auancez, que ie nomme mes nouueaux Amis; i'en ay d'autres que
> i'apelle simplement mes Amis: i'en ay aussi que ie puis
> apeller des Amis d'habitude: i'en ay quelques-vns que ie
> nomme de solides Amis: & quelques autres que i'apelle mes
> Amis particuliers; mais pour ceux que ie mets au rang de mes
> tendres Amis, ils sont en fort petit nombre; & ils sont si
> auant dans mon coeur, qu'on n'y peut iamais faire plus de
> progrés (I, 390f).

Herminius asks which category he belongs to, and, when told that
he is at *Nouvelle-Amitié*, asks the way to *Tendre*; it is in
response to this request that Clélie promises 'de vous donner la
Carte de ce Païs' (I, 392ff). Clélie does not implement her
promise immediately, thinking that her friends will not take her
seriously; the next morning, however, she receives a letter from
Herminius, repeating his request. This time Clélie immediately
complies: 'si bien que sans hesiter vn moment, elle prit des
Tablettes, & escriuit ce qu'elle auoit si agreablement imaginé: &

elle l'executa si viste, qu'en vne demie heure elle eut commencé, & acheué ce qu'elle auoit pensé' (I, 395f). Herminius's function, like that of Pellisson at the beginning of his relationship with Mlle de Scudéry, is not to create new attitudes, but to crystallize and give expression to existing ones; there is already a group of *tendres amis* to which Aronce has been seeking admission before Herminius's arrival, just as there is a group round Mlle de Scudéry which has to decide whether or not to allow Pellisson to join its ranks.

The similarity between Herminius and Pellisson, already obvious in their function as catalysts, is emphasized also in other ways. The fictional character, for example, travels from Rome at the prompting of his mother, just as the historical figure had made the journey from Castres to Paris.[3] Moreover, Mlle de Scudéry takes care to point out that Herminius is in love with someone in Rome, just as Pellisson, at the time of seeking entry to Mlle de Scudéry's circle, was actively courting Geneviève Perricquet. This similarity allows Mlle de Scudéry to evoke, behind the transparent veil of fiction, something of her own relationship with Pellisson, and to insist that that relationship is one of *amitié* rather than *amour*. What Herminius seeks of Clélie is not incompatible with loving elsewhere, although it is admitted that this is an exceptional case; it is unusual 'que ceux qui ont vne violente amour, puissent auoir en mesme temps vne violente amitié'. Indeed, the persistence of Herminius is such that it could easily give rise to misunderstanding; had it not been known that he had a mistress elsewhere, 'nous eussions creû qu'il estoit amoureux de Clélie: car il la loüoit auec vne certaine exageration, qui semble estre particuliere à l'amour; il la cherchoit auec vn soin extréme; il estoit rauy de ioye quand il estoit aupres d'elle; il s'ennuyoit quand il ne la voyoit pas' (I, 387f). Both Herminius and Aronce, in their own different ways, illustrate that in fiction, as in life, the *pays de Tendre* lies close enough to the land of love to be easily mistaken for it (Herminius) or to be some kind of substitute for it (Aronce); in

both cases, however, it is clear that the *pays de Tendre* remains
an independent kingdom.

It is of course possible, as Niderst suggests, that in
transposing her relationship with Pellisson into the fictional
mode, Mlle de Scudéry is simply trying to present that
relationship in the best possible light.[4] It is certainly true
that *Clélie* is not merely a representation but an embellishment of
life in Mlle de Scudéry's circle. The character of Clélie can
hardly be said to be a faithful portrait of Mlle de Scudéry
herself; the plain, forty-six year old authoress has become
metamorphosed into a youthful beauty who has only to appear in
order to conquer all hearts, and who is being actively sought by
two different suitors. Yet the dominant impression which emerges
from Mlle de Scudéry's treatment of the *Carte de Tendre* in *Clélie*
is not so much one of an idealizing tendency as of a serious
polemical intention, a desire to put an end to misunderstandings
and to set the record straight. From the beginning, Clélie is
uneasy about the possibility of knowledge of the *Carte de Tendre*
spreading beyond a limited circle, for inevitably, she thinks, it
will be seized upon by people incapable of understanding what it
is meant to represent: '... elle ne vouloit pas que de sottes
Gens, qui ne sçauroient pas le commencement de la chose, & qui ne
seroient pas capables d'entendre cette nouuelle galanterie,
allassent en parler selon leur caprice, ou la grossiereté de leur
esprit' (I, 406). The *Carte de Tendre*, however, becomes widely
known, and indeed causes something of a sensation among polite
society in Capua. When this happens, Clélie again expresses her
apprehension, this time to Herminius; she is afraid that if the
public comes to know of something that has been created 'pour
nostre Cabale en particulier', people will take seriously what is
only 'vne follie d'vn moment, que ie ne regarde tout au plus que
comme vne bagatelle ...' (I, 407ff). Her fears are allayed to
some extent by the reception given to the *Carte de Tendre*, which
meets with the approval of most of society, apart, that is, from
'quelques Gens grossiers, stupides, malicieux, ou mauuais
Plaisans' (I, 409). From remarks such as these, it would appear

that Mlle de Scudéry is signalling to her readers over the heads
of her characters, expressing something of her own irritation at
the misunderstandings to which the *Carte de Tendre* has given rise
among some at least of her contemporaries, and taking the
opportunity provided by the fictional use of the *Carte de Tendre*
to explain what the significance of the allegory is.

One of the methods which Mlle de Scudéry uses in order to
clarify her intention is to accompany the *Carte de Tendre* with a
fairly detailed commentary, given by Celere, the narrator of the
story of Aronce and Clélie. Celere's commentary is largely a
description in words of what the *Carte de Tendre* says more
concisely in pictorial form. Some of Celere's remarks are of
interest, however, particularly those which deal with the various
routes by which one may pass from *Nouvelle-Amitié* to *Tendre*. The
speediest route is of course by the river of *Inclination*; the fact
that there are no stopping places along the river signifies 'que
la tendresse qui naist par inclination, n'a besoin de rien autre
chose pour estre ce qu'elle est' (I, 400). As far as the other
routes are concerned, Celere emphasizes the progressive nature of
the journey. One must pass through the various *étapes* in the
order given; for instance, after *Petits-Soins*, one must progress
to *Assiduité*, 'pour faire entendre que ce n'est pas assez d'auoir
durant quelques iours tous ces petits soins' (I, 402). Thus, each
*étape* represents an attitude which both complements and qualifies
those around it. Although on the map one progresses from one
stage to the next, in the development of an actual relationship
none of the qualities necessary for *tendre amitié* is ever left
behind; the journey to *Tendre* is not only progressive but
cumulative. The unknown territory beyond the *pays de Tendre* is
quite specifically identified with love. The *Mer Dangereuse* is so
called because 'il est assez dangereux à vne Femme, d'aller vn peu
au delà des dernieres bornes de l'amitié', and the presence on the
map of the *Terres Inconnues* signifies that Clélie 'n'a point eu
d'amour, & qu'elle n'en peut auoir' (I, 405); she is unable
therefore to speak of these regions from first-hand experience.
In this way, Celere's exegesis of the *Carte de Tendre* points in

the same direction as Clélie's fears of misunderstanding and the insistence that Herminius is seeking Clélie's friendship and not her love; yet again, it is clear that while *tendresse* may resemble love, it is nevertheless distinct from it.

As if anxious to make absolutely sure that the reader of *Clélie* has grasped this crucial distinction, Mlle de Scudéry underlines it in yet another way. The impact made on the plot of the romance by the *Carte de Tendre* is not confined to the point at which the map is created and discussed. As we have seen, the *Carte de Tendre* is drawn up by Clélie for Herminius; it is natural therefore for it to feature not only in the story of Aronce and Clélie, but also in the 'Histoire d'Herminius & de Valerie', recounted in a later volume. In the story of Herminius, the *Carte de Tendre* gives rise to an episode in which Valerie becomes jealous, mistakenly thinking that Herminius is in love with Clélie. What prompts the mistake is the exchange between Herminius and Clélie of 'tous ces billets d'amitié galante, qui sembloient des billets d'amour à la malheureuse Valerie' (V, 460), and more important still the *Carte de Tendre*, which Valerie misinterprets: 'Elle vit la Carte de Tendre comme vne Carte d'amour, plustost que comme vne Carte d'amitié' (V, 555). In coming to this conclusion, Valerie is merely repeating the mistake of another character called Emile, who has described to Valerie the relationship between Herminius and Clélie, and who has imagined 'que la Carte de Tendre estoit vne Carte de l'amour vertueuse' (I, 425). Herminius eventually succeeds in convincing Valerie that in spite of appearances, he and Clélie are not lovers but *tendres amis*. It goes without saying that any reader who may still be tempted to make Valerie's mistake about the significance of the *Carte de Tendre* is expected to follow her on the road to enlightenment.

The chief method by which Mlle de Scudéry makes explicit her intentions regarding the *Carte de Tendre* is not by the various repercussions which the episode has on the plot, but rather by the inclusion of a passage which has already been mentioned, namely the discussion of *tendresse* which takes place before Clélie and her family leave Carthage (I, 202-21). By its position, this discussion is very obviously intended to prepare the reader for the *Carte de Tendre* episode which comes a little later, and the fact that the main participants in the discussion are none other than Aronce and Clélie themselves adds to the authoritativeness of the opinions expressed. In addition, the *tendresse* discussion may be said to present in a concise form a number of issues which Mlle de Scudéry takes up and amplifies elsewhere. For these reasons it is appropriate to study it in some detail.

## 3. *The Tendresse Discussion*

The *tendresse* discussion involves not only Aronce and Clélie, but also Horace, Barcé, Sozonisbe and Celere, who will later recount it. It turns essentially on the question of whether the epithet *tendre* may be applied only to *amitié*, or to *amour* as well. Clélie finds the expression *tendre amitié* perfectly acceptable, but *tendre amour* strikes her as being odd: 'Ie comprends bien, repliqua Clelie, qu'on peut dire vne amitié tendre; & qu'il y a mesme vne notable difference entre vne amitié ordinaire, & vne tendre amitié; mais ... ie n'ay iamais entendu dire vne tendre amour' (I, 203). The fact that disagreement exists over what is acceptable current usage prompts Celere to stress the need for the word *tendre* to be defined, because, as he puts it, 'tant de gens s'en seruent auiourd'huy ... qu'on ne sçaura bien tost plus sa veritable signification' (I, 203); in Carthage, as in Paris, *tendre* has clearly become part of fashionable jargon. Aronce urges that the definition be given by Clélie, who obviously knows the value of *tendresse* in friendship; once he has heard her definition, he will undertake to convince her that *tendresse* is equally appropriate in love. From this way of presenting the discussion - the emphasis on the need for a definition and the fact that the definition should be placed in the mouth of the romance's heroine - it is as if Mlle de Scudéry herself, conscious of the different meanings given to the word *tendre*, is anxious to explain what she, as the author of the *Carte de Tendre* and therefore the originator of the new term, conceives *tendresse* to be.

Before attempting a formal definition of *tendresse*, Clélie, returning to a distinction which she has already established, explains the difference between 'vne amitié ordinaire, & vne tendre amitié'. The distinguishing mark of the former is that, lacking *tendresse*, it involves the emotions only at a very superficial level; it is 'vne espece d'amitié tranquille, qui ne donne ny de grandes douceurs, ny de grandes inquietudes, à ceux qui en sont capables' (I, 206). In *amitié ordinaire*, the presence of the object of friendship is sought only half-heartedly, and his absence tolerated without difficulty. Moreover, such friends remain relatively unmoved by each other's misfortunes, and do not defend each other when attacked. They tend to seek their own interests, rather than the interests of the other; they are fair-weather friends, readily abandoning each other in adversity. Their friendship is of the head rather than the heart. 'La generosité & la vanité ont autant de part à tout ce qu'ils font que l'amitié'; that is to say, when they perform the duties of a friend, it is as a result of a conscious decision to do so, and with self-glorification in mind.[5] This description which Clélie gives of *amitié ordinaire* meets with the approval of the other participants in the discussion; Sozonisbe quotes an example of a friend who has abandoned her, and Horace remarks that 'pour l'ordinaire on se contente de pleindre les malheureux sans les secourir' (I, 210); in *amitié ordinaire*, involvement in the other's situation is less than total. *Tendre amitié*, on the other hand, as Clélie goes on to make clear, is altogether a more satisfying affair. The presence of *tendresse* gives to friendship 'ie ne sçay quel carractere de galanterie qui la rend plus diuertissante; elle inspire la ciuilité & l'exactitude à ceux qui en sont capables' (I, 210). *Tendresse* begins in increased attention to politeness, to the normal courtesies of everyday life; ordinary social exchanges provide the most commonly met with situation in which concern for the well being of the other is called for, and the forms of polite behaviour demanded by these exchanges are an obvious vehicle for this concern to express itself.

While it involves the social niceties, *tendresse* is a much wider concept, as Clélie demonstrates when finally, after having explained the difference *tendresse* makes to friendship, she goes on to propose a definition:

> Mais pour bien definir la tendresse, ie pense pouuoir dire, que c'est vne certaine sensibilité de coeur, qui ne se trouue presques iamais souuerainement, qu'en des personnes qui ont l'ame noble, les inclinations vertueuses, & l'esprit bien tourné; & qui fait que lorsqu'elles ont de l'amitié, elles l'ont sincere, & ardente; & qu'elles sentent si vivement toutes les douleurs, & toutes les ioyes de ceux qu'elles aiment, qu'elles ne sentent pas tant les leurs propres (I, 211).

In order to be *tendre*, Clélie is saying, the necessary qualification is a particularly heightened ability to experience emotion, to respond to a situation through feeling rather than through the intellect. Her use of the phrase 'sensibilité de coeur' has an almost eighteenth-century ring about it, for she makes it plain that this *sensibilité* is the hallmark of an élite; it is associated with a noble soul, a desire to do right, and a well formed mind, and therefore sets its possessor apart from ordinary mortals. In the last clause of her definition, Clélie explains the relationship between *sensibilité* and *tendresse*. When people are equipped with *sensibilité*, they bring to friendship the ability to recreate vicariously the emotions of the other, to project themselves empathically into one another's joys and sorrows, to experience the world as the other experiences it. *Sensibilité* thus allows an identification with the other, a sharing which, as Clélie says, leads to self-forgetfulness; and the close fellowship which is created in this way is the essence of *tendresse*. It is a question not so much of loving one's neighbour as oneself, as of feeling what it is like to be him. The *ami ordinaire* remains unmoved by his friend's emotions; the *ami tendre* assumes them totally.

The corollary of this ability to feel one's way into the joys and sorrows of someone else is of course that because of it one will tend quite naturally to avoid what gives the other pain and seek what gives the other pleasure, as if the other were a kind of second self. In this way, *tendresse* is at the opposite pole to self-interest; it actively seeks the good of the other, preferring what is conducive to the other's well-being and happiness to self-aggrandizement and self-gratification. This self-forgetfulness underlies various kinds of behaviour which Clélie says are characteristic of *tendres amis*: preferring to be with an unfortunate friend rather than amusing oneself, excusing a friend's faults and praising his virtues, rendering 'les grands services' without at the same time neglecting 'les petits soins' (I, 212). Yet, paradoxically perhaps, the reward for such self-effacement is great satisfaction for the individual; Clélie describes the joy of *tendres amis* as being of a particularly exquisite kind. This joy comes from having given joy to the other, as for example when 'ceux qui ont vne amitié tendre ... escoutent vne parole obligeante, auec vne ioye qui oblige ceux qui la leur ont dite' (I, 213). In those who are the recipients of acts of consideration, the reaction is not only joy but gratitude: 'ils sçauent gré des plus petites choses' (I, 213). A manifestation of *tendresse*, an example of setting the other's interest before one's own, thus evokes not only joy - in the recipient, and hence, vicariously, in the doer - but also, in the recipient, *reconnaissance*, which prompts him to wish to return the favour he has received. In this way, *tendresse* is self-perpetuating, since its presence in one partner calls it forth in the other, who, by his reaction, shows that he was worthy to receive *tendresse* in the first place. *Tendresse* offers the possibility of a stable and lasting relationship, one which lends itself to constant renewal. Clélie is in no doubt that it is *tendresse* which provides 'toute la douceur, & toute la perfection de l'amitié', and which so transforms *amitié* that 'sans tenir rien du desreglement de l'amour, elle luy ressemble pourtant en beaucoup de choses' (I, 212). Here we have at least part of the explanation of the geographical location of the *pays de Tendre*, situated as it is near the land of love without being part of it; as Clélie conceives it, *tendre amitié*, while being safer and more controlled than love, nevertheless offers some of the same rewards. In stressing these rewards, Clélie in a sense is coming back to the point of departure of her definition of *tendresse*: the same *sensibilité* which makes *tendre amitié* possible is also what stands to gain most from it.

Clélie's view of *tendre amitié* as a kind of substitute for love is of course coloured by the fact that at this particular moment in the story, love is for her still a *terre inconnue*. Nevertheless, her point about the similarity of the rewards offered by *tendre amitié* and *amour* is in line with Mlle de Scudéry's insistence that these two areas of experience, while in some ways similar, are not the same. Further light on the rather ambivalent relationship between *tendresse* and *amour* is shed by Aronce, who in fulfilment of his promise sets out to prove that *tendresse* is just as necessary for the lover as it is for the friend. Indeed, Aronce argues, *tendresse* is even more necessary for the lover, and the reason for this lies in a fundamental difference between *amitié* and *amour*. *Amitié* is an 'affection qui naist presques tousiours auec l'aide de la raison' (I, 216), and this essential rationality which is preserved in friendship makes it possible to decide to act as if one were *tendre*, even if one is not naturally so; love on the other hand is 'presques tousiours incomparable [*sic*] auec la raison' (I, 215f). Like Clélie with her talk of 'desreglement', Aronce sees love as an unruly, uncontrollable passion with a natural tendency towards disorder. Left to itself, this natural tendency would prevail and would lead to unbridled selfishness, to an attempt on the part of the lover to use the beloved merely as an instrument of his own gratification. The function of *tendresse* in love is precisely to counteract this downward pull. It can function in this way because its essence is self-forgetfulness: 'vn des Principaux effets de la veritable tendresse', remarks Aronce, echoing Clélie's earlier definition, 'c'est qu'elle fait qu'on pense beaucoup plus à l'interest de ce qu'on aime, qu'au sien propre' (I, 216). This means that a love which lacks *tendresse* cannot be said to be an enriching and ennobling experience, but positively demeans both the lover and the beloved. Aronce insists that 'vne amour sans tendresse, n'a que des desirs impetueux, qui n'ont ny bornes, ny retenuë', because the lover 'ne considere que sa propre satisfaction, sans considerer la gloire de la Personne aimée', and seeks only 'tout ce qui luy peut plaire sans reserue' (I, 216). In *amour* as in *amitié*, *tendresse* stands at the opposite pole to self-interest, and, put simply, Aronce's argument is that *tendresse* is more necessary in love because by the nature of things self-interest is potentially a more serious problem.

Having announced his basic proposition, Aronce amplifies it by describing, as Clélie had earlier done in her discussion of *amitié*, the differences which the presence or absence of *tendresse* can make to love. Just as Clélie sees the first sign of *tendresse* as increased attention to social niceties, so for Aronce the first indication of the absence of *tendresse* in lovers is that their manners suffer, and their relationships become awkward and uncomfortable: 'en effet, ces Amans fiers qui sont ennemis de la tendresse, & qui en medisent, sont ordinairement insolens, inciuils, pleins de vanité, aisez à fascher, difficiles à apaiser, indiscrets quand on les fauorise, & insuportables quand on les mal-traite' (I, 216f). Like *amis ordinaires*, too, lovers who lack *tendresse* live lives which from the point of view of the range of feelings of which they are capable, are superficial and restricted. Such lovers set no store by 'toutes ces petites choses qui donnent de si grands & de si sensibles plaisirs, à ceux qui ont l'ame tendre'; they read letters from their mistress only once, and experience no 'agitation' when they meet her; they are unable either to 'resuer' or 'soupirer agreablement', being strangers to 'vne certaine melancolie douce qui naist de la tendresse d'vn coeur amoureux, & qui l'occupe quelquesfois plus doucement, que la ioye ne le pourroit faire' (I, 217f). This inability to feel leads them to the mistaken belief that the 'despenses excessiues' in which they engage are sufficient proof of love (I, 218). In other words, lack of *tendresse* does not only lead to behaviour characterized principally by self-seeking, but involves also a lack of discernment and insight. The *amant tendre*, on the other hand, is both morally and sentimentally superior to his counterpart who lacks *tendresse*. 'Ie pose mesme pour fondement', argues Aronce, 'qu'vn Amant tendre ne sçauroit estre, ny infidelle, ny fourbe, ny vain, ny insolent, ny indiscret' (I, 221); that is, *tendresse* guarantees both the security and the permanence of the relationship. The sentimental superiority of the *amant tendre*, however, is if anything even more marked. Aronce makes the point that while most other positive qualities may be acquired, and negative ones eradicated, by dint of conscious effort, the same cannot be said of *tendresse*, described as 'vn present des Dieux, dont ils ne sont iamais prodigues', (I, 219f). A lover who lacks *tendresse* may of course decide to act as though he possessed it, although such an attempt must inevitably fail, because 'ceux qui se connoissent en tendresse, ne s'y sçauroient iamais tromper' (I, 220). Thus, *tendresse* sets its possessor apart from ordinary lovers, marks him out as belonging to a small, privileged élite. As well as their many other advantages, members of this exclusive group have the ability to identify each other; *tendresse* confers unerring judgment of character, and this recognition by both partners that the other is a kindred spirit further strengthens the bond which mutual *tendresse* is already capable of creating.

One may say then that from Clélie and Aronce's discussion of the importance of *tendresse* in *amitié* and *amour* respectively, a number of key points emerge. These may be recapitulated briefly. *Tendresse* is essentially a function of *sensibilité* in that it involves the ability to project oneself empathically into the other's situation, to feel for and with the other; it is consequently a tendency which works in the opposite direction to self-interest. This means that from the moral point of view it is so to speak positively charged, conducing to virtue, whereas the negative force of self-interest tends to undermine the moral worth of human behaviour. As well as favouring goodness, *tendresse* contributes also to happiness; the *sensibilité* which is the necessary precondition for *tendresse* receives its reward in kind, in an extended range of feeling, and in access to sources of joy which are not available to the uninitiated. *Tendresse* brings with it membership of an élite; individuals who belong to this group are linked by a kind of elective affinity, and the *tendresse* which exists in relationships between such individuals is self-perpetuating in that a display of it will call forth in the other a desire to reciprocate. Finally, as far as the relative positions of *tendresse* and *amour* are concerned, Aronce's and Clélie's discussion brings out very clearly both the similarities and the essential difference. *Tendresse* is not synonymous with *amour* or for that matter with *amitié*; it is rather a basic attitude of identification with others which is equally appropriate in the non-sexual context of friendship and the more explicitly sexual one of love. In both of these contexts, *tendresse* can act as a safeguard against the disruptive effects which are felt to accompany love. For Clélie, *tendre amitié* is a safer substitute for love; Aronce does not fundamentally disagree with her, but argues that the protective effect of *tendresse* can operate equally well within the context of love as outside it. Love's potential for disorder is neutralized by *tendresse*, and love is thus legitimized, made compatible with high standards of behaviour and the attainment of a high level of happiness.

The question arises of how far the opinions expressed by Aronce and Clélie in the course of their discussion can be attributed to Mlle de Scudéry herself. If the *tendresse* discussion is looked at in the context of the ideas expressed by Mlle de Scudéry elsewhere, it very quickly becomes clear that the main themes of the discussion coincide with some of Mlle de Scudéry's major preoccupations. No exhaustive treatment exists of the many facets of the complex vision which is articulated in Mlle de Scudéry's work as a whole, and no such treatment can be attempted here. Some account needs to be given, however, of the ideas expressed elsewhere by Mlle de Scudéry on issues raised by Aronce and Clélie, since these ideas contribute to a more complete understanding of the *tendresse* discussion and hence of the *Carte de Tendre* itself.

## 4. Tendresse in Mlle de Scudéry's Thought

The concept of *tendresse* which emerges from Clélie and Aronce's discussion is one which occupies an important place in Mlle de Scudéry's thinking even before the publication of *Clélie*. If, as Clélie suggests, the *Carte de Tendre* was only half an hour in the making, the attitudes which it reflects crystallized over a much longer period. As early as 1647, for example, there is a significant passage in a letter written to Mlle Dumoulin in which Mlle de Scudéry states that in ordinary friendship, one must wait a long time before receiving 'de grands témoignages de générosité et de tendresse'; by contrast, Mlle Dumoulin's friendship has from the beginning been 'officieuse, agissante et libérale jusques à tel point qu'elle donne ce que l'on doit préférer à tous les trésors et à toutes les richesses imaginables'.[6] Even without a map, it would seem, Mlle Dumoulin has arrived at *Tendre* by the river of *Inclination*, the route which involves no stops on the way. Six years before the composition of the *Carte de Tendre*, the relative expeditiousness of different routes to *Tendre* is clearly in Mlle de Scudéry's mind.

The views expressed by Clélie and Aronce concerning the protection afforded by *tendresse* against the disorders to which love is liable appear to represent one of the major articles in Mlle de Scudéry's own creed. Towards the end of *Le Grand Cyrus*, there is an intercalated *histoire* which probably provides a better insight than anything else written before *Clélie* into Mlle de Scudéry's thinking on *tendresse* and its relationship with *amitié* and *amour*. In the 'Histoire de Sapho', Mlle de Scudéry uses the character of Sapho to present what is very obviously a self-portrait - idealized no doubt, but clearly recognizable - and the result is that the opinions which Sapho expresses carry a greal deal of weight. Sapho is just as aware as Aronce and Clélie will be later of love's potential for disrupting a life, but her defence of love is more direct and explicit. She is sympathetic up to a point with those who say that a woman should avoid love altogether because of the 'fâcheuses suites' it can have (*Cyrus*, X, 412); at the same time she argues that the urge to love is planted in us by the gods and therefore should be given some place in the scheme of things. The 'déreglemens' of love come from the character of the lover rather than from the nature of love itself; in those capable of responding appropriately, 'cét agreable eschange de pensées, & de pensées secrettes, qui se font entre deux Personnes qui s'aiment, est vn plaisir inconceuable' (*Cyrus*, X, 413). As in the case of Clélie, later, it is emphasized that Sapho is not talking of love from personal experience, but rather extrapolating from what she knows of friendship. It later transpires that the mutual identification and sharing which Sapho sees as the hallmark of *amitié* is something of which she *has* had direct personal experience. The 'Histoire de Sapho' contains an account of the relationship between Sapho and a character named Phaon, who is a literary transcription of Pellisson, just as Sapho is of Mlle de Scudéry herself. This relationship is *amitié*, not *amour*, but *amitié* marked by very close communion. 'Ils se disoient toutes leurs pensées: ils les entendoient mesme sans se les dire: ils voyoient dans leurs yeux tous les mouuemens de leurs coeurs: & ils y voyoient des sentimens si tendres, que plus ils se connoissoint [*sic*], plus ils s'aimoient' (*Cyrus*, X, 504). Into the mouth of Phaon, Mlle de Scudéry places a declaration of faith in the permanence of *tendresse*, in the power of the *tendre coeur* to reverse the mutability of time. 'Car enfin', Phaon declares, 'les yeux s'accoustument à la beauté, & ce qu'on a veû long temps, n'a plus la grace que la nouueauté donne: mais la tendresse d'vn coeur amoureux & passionné, est vne source inespuisable de nouueaux plaisirs, qui naissent en foule de moment en moment: & qui augmentent l'amour auec le temps; au lieu que pour l'ordinaire le temps la diminuë' (*Cyrus*, X, 469). Passages such as these already contain in germ some of the main ideas which Aronce and Clélie will later develop - the emphasis on the sharing of experience, the recognition by each partner that the other belongs to the same élite, the ability of *tendresse* to renew itself. If Pellisson has arrived at *Tendre*, it is because he has proved that he matches the ideal which Mlle de Scudéry consistently uses as a yardstick.

Although they may have been in existence earlier, the ideas expressed in the *tendresse* discussion on the relationship of *tendresse* to *amitié* and *amour* are most fully worked out in *Clélie*, which most directly represents the spirit of the *samedis* group. It is certainly true that it is *Clélie* which most explicitly formulates the connection between *tendresse* and *sensibilité*, and which provides the clearest indication of what the term *sensibilité* implied for Mlle de Scudéry. *Tendresse* and *sensibilité* are qualities which tend to be associated within the same character; they are part of the hero's equipment, in friendship as in love. Of Aronce it is said, in the portrait of him near the beginning of *Clélie*, that he possesses 'l'ame tendre, le coeur sensible; il aime ses Amis comme luy mesme; il les sert auec ardeur' (I, 69). These are qualities which he carries over into his love for Clélie; later in the work we see him greet her, after a long absence, 'auec tout le transport qu'vne veritable amour peut donner à vn Amant qui a le coeur tendre & sensible' (VIII, 1165). Secondary characters too illustrate the nature of the relationship between *sensibilité* and *tendresse*. Particularly instructive in this respect is the case of Melinthe, a mother who, 'poussée par vne veritable tendresse de mere', does not hesitate to put her own life at risk in saving her children when their house comes under enemy fire (*Clélie*, VIII, 1307). We are not told directly of Melinthe's *sensibilité*, but later in the work a contrast is drawn between her and another character named Hersilie, who 'n'a point le coeur sensible' (X, 876). Interestingly, Hersilie's lack of *sensibilité* shows itself in the absence of an ability which Melinthe herself possesses to the full, that of being touched by the 'charmes de la solitude'; Hersilie reproaches Melinthe for taking 'plus de plaisir à voir passer de ses fenestres de grands bateaux chargez de diuerses choses rustiques, que de voir quelque magnifique course de cheuaux' (X, 876f). In her possession of this quality, Melinthe appears to embody views expressed earlier in a discussion concerning attitudes towards animals, both tame and wild. In this discussion it is argued that a man's attitude towards animals is a mark of what kind of man he is. 'I'ay tousiours remarqué', affirms one of the characters who appears to command widespread support from the assembled company to which she is speaking, 'que les hommes cruels haïssent les bestes, & qu'ordinairement les bonnes personnes les aiment, ou ne peuuent du moins souffrir qu'on leur fasse mal. Mais pour ces Gents ambitieux, qui sont si satisfaits d'eux mesmes, & qui ne peuuent penser qu'à de grandes choses, ils n'ont garde de s'amuser à regarder le nid d'vne Arondelle [sic], à admirer le trauail des Fourmis, le chant des Rossignols, l'amour des Tourterelles, & l'amitié des chiens ...' (VIII, 963). In other words, love of nature points to an emotional sensitivity which is enjoyed by only a few, and at the same time to the self-forgetfulness and identification with the other which is so prized in friendship and love alike. *Sensibilité* may find its principal manifestation in human relationships, but it is not confined to them; it is a general tendency to respond to the world not through the head, but through the heart.

Throughout *Clélie*, there is a constant reiteration of the idea that the *sensibilité* which makes *tendresse* possible is a rare quality, one which is conspicuously lacking in society at large. This is the case in both of the areas, friendship and love, in which *tendresse* normally expresses itself. As far as friendship is concerned, for example, Aronce's friend Amilcar stresses the difficulty of becoming 'amis de bonne foy', that is, friends 'qui sentent toutes les douleurs de ceux qu'ils aiment, qui entrent dans tous leurs interests sans exception' (IX, 488). Amilcar's statement comes in support of Plotine, who is close to expressing complete disillusionment with mankind, believing as she does that 'tout le monde n'est que feinte', and that 'ceux en qui on se fie le plus, sont ceux dont on est le plus trompé', (IX, 486); in this way the self-interest which is at the opposite pole to *tendresse* is associated with the problem of social falsity, the decision people take to wear a mask in order to deceive others and thus further their own interests. In the last volume of *Clélie* Mlle de Scudéry throws her own weight behind her characters' assessment of

the rarity of *tendresse*; in an authorial comment, she expresses
identical sentiments to those of Amilcar, in almost identical
words. 'Il n'y a sans doute qu'vn tres-petit nombre de personnes
qui soient assez genereuses pour entrer de bonne foy dans les
interests de tous ceux qu'ils aiment, & dont le coeur soit assez
sensible pour estre penetré de la douleur d'autruy', (X, 550);
again the emphasis is on total sharing – the treating of the
other's interests as if they were one's own, which comes from
compassion (in the original sense of suffering with the other) –
and on how exceptional it is to find this ability. 'Il y a cent
mille personnes', exclaims another character earlier in the work,
'qui croyent aimer, & qui n'aiment pas: & qui apellent amitié vne
espece de société où le commerce de la vie oblige necessairement.
Mais quand ie parle d'amitié, i'entens parler d'vne amitié
effectiue, tendre, & solide tout ensemble, d'vne amitié ou il se
fait vn eschange de coeurs, & de secrets; & dont la tendresse est
extréme' (IV, 906). Clearly, friendship based on empathic
identification is conceived as an ideal which is only very
occasionally realized in everyday life.

In the case of love, the effects of the rarity of *tendresse*
are if anything more marked. It will be recalled that for Aronce,
*tendresse* is even more important in *amour* than in *amitié*, since
without it love 'n'a que des desirs impetueux, qui n'ont ny
bornes, ny retenuë' (I, 216). In the course of a long discussion,
later in *Clélie*, of *amitié* and *amour*, Herminius returns to the
same theme, likening love to the River Tiber, which, he says,
receives the waters of forty-two tributaries; if it merely
consisted of the waters of its source, it would be nothing more
than a paltry stream. In the same way, he argues, love in its
proper sense, that of the attraction between the sexes, would by
itself be a very little thing, shallow and quickly dried up; it
only becomes a broad majestic river when joined by 'tout ce qui
est nécessaire aux grandes & belles amitiez' (V, 323f). Again,
this is an ideal which contrasts markedly with what can be
observed to happen in the majority of relationships. In a
criticism of court life, we are told that what passes for love

between courtiers is not worthy of the name; 'pour de l'amour il y en a peu qu'on puisse appeller amour; on y trouue pourtant quelquefois de certaines amours friuoles, qui ne sont propres qu'à de ieunes oysifs qui ne sçauent que faire, & qui mesme bien souuent ne sçauent que dire. On y voit des amours d'interests, qui n'inspirent que de lasches actions, & l'on n'y voit presques iamais d'amours sinceres' (VIII, 1389f). Self-interest thus gives rise to a love which is superficial, morally demeaning rather than uplifting, and which is associated once more, as in the case of Plotine, with insincerity and sham. This 'love' which characterizes the court, however, is not unique, but represents a particular case of what is a widespread attitude. A hermit who after a wide experience of the world has withdrawn from society because of the 'foiblesse, folie, iniustice & meschanceté' which he has everywhere observed, despairs of finding 'deux personnes qui s'aiment, qui ayent l'esprit assez grand, le coeur assez tendre, & l'ame assez constante pour s'aymer tousiours'; yet without these qualities, love 'n'est que foiblesse, crime, & folie' (X, 709). Herminius too takes up the idea of *amours frivoles*, contrasting their superficiality with the solid delights of a love based on *tendresse*. 'Au reste', he exclaims, 'quand ie parle de l'amour, ie n'entends pas parler de ces amours friuoles qui portent vn nom qu'elles ne meritent pas, car ceux qui s'aiment de cette sorte ... ne s'engagent à rien qu'à se diuertir le mieux qu'ils pourront, tant qu'ils auront la fantaisie de se voir & de s'aimer. Mais i'entends parler d'vne certaine amour ardente & sincere ... où il se fait vn veritable eschange de coeurs, où les volontez se confondent, & qui semble deuoir durer eternellement' (VII, 113-4). Here, Herminius, like Phaon in *Le Grand Cyrus* - a not unsurprising similarity, since both characters are modelled on Pellisson - is concerned above all with the permanence of love; the presence of *tendresse*, which, as we have seen, is self-renewing, maximizes not only the intensity of love's pleasures, but also their duration. *Amour-tendresse* cheats time by establishing an area of fixity and stability in a world in which the vast bulk of relationships are particularly susceptible to change and decay.

Passages such as those quoted above suggest that Mlle de Scudéry's concept of *tendresse* contains within it an element of social criticism, that it is prompted by her observations of her contemporaries and a certain dissatisfaction with their behaviour, that it is a protest against the various forms of *galanterie*. The impression that Mlle de Scudéry sees herself in some degree as a crusader, attempting to find a remedy for what she considers to be the deficiencies of current norms of behaviour, receives striking confirmation from another source. There is preserved in Mlle de Scudéry's correspondence an exchange of letters with Mlle Descartes; the letters are undated, but from the sentiments expressed would seem to belong to a relatively late stage in Mlle de Scudéry's long career. Mlle Descartes writes that a study of Mlle de Scudéry's works has inspired in her an aversion to love as it commonly manifests itself in society of the time: 'Vos beaux livres m'ont fait connoître/Un amour généreux, pur et sans intérêt,/Et qui l'a vu tel qu'il doit être/Ne peut le souffrir comme il est'. In her reply, Mlle de Scudéry reveals that her description of ideal love has been prompted by a desire to end the reign of what she calls 'vulgaires amours', but the desire has remained unfulfilled: 'Mais malgré cet espoir nous voyons mille coeurs/Se laisser conquérir par d'indignes vainqueurs'. Her ideal of love, she continues, has been conceived as a 'contre-poison' to such relationships; she has painted a picture of 'ce qu'Amour a de beau/Par l'opposition des amours passagères,/Des amours d'intérêt, des amours mensongères,/Des sentiments grossiers et de leurs faux appas'.[7] The 'opposition' mentioned in the last stanza represents the same fundamental polarity which may be discerned in Mlle de Scudéry's work as a whole. On the one hand, there are the *vulgaires amours*, the *amours frivoles*, those of society at large; at their root is self-interest, from which they derive both their impermanence and their insincerity, and they are consequently morally demeaning, linked with disorder. On the other hand, there is *amour-tendresse*, the self-denying identification with the situation of the other, dependent on a *sensibilité* which simultaneously guarantees the permanence and the authenticity of a relationship, allowing it to be morally elevating, preventing disorder, and giving unrivalled potential as a source of happiness. Self-interest and *tendresse* are the basic categories under which all relationships may be subsumed. There is either love of self or true love of the other; a given relationship can depend on one or the other, but not on both at the same time.

To highlight the importance of *tendresse* in this way is not of course to deny that Mlle de Scudéry's proposed solution to the problems of contemporary behaviour has other elements besides *sensibilité*. Again and again in her work she returns to the idea that happiness through social relationships depends not only on a heightened sensitivity to emotion, but also on moral worth as evidenced by the practice of the traditional virtues, and on gifts of mind and intellect - the kind of gifts which add a certain spice to social intercourse and conversation. Yet it is clear that for Mlle de Scudéry, the greatest of all these is *sensibilité*. Clélie, in her definition of *tendresse*, insists, it will be remembered, that *sensibilité* can only be found at its highest in 'des personnes qui ont l'ame noble, les inclinations vertueuses, & l'esprit bien tourné' (I, 211); that is, intellectual and moral qualities are important not so much on their own account as for the fact that they provide a suitable climate in which *sensibilité* may come to full fruition. It is also possible, as Aronce in the same discussion shows, to conceive of the link between *sensibilité* and these other valued qualities as working in the opposite direction. In his argument for the importance of *tendresse* in love, Aronce makes it clear that he thinks of the qualities in question as stemming from and being guaranteed by *sensibilité*; a man or a woman is morally upright and possesses the social graces *because* he or she is *sensible*. For both Clélie and Aronce, however, the association between qualities and *sensibilité* is a close one. Like the bad tree of self-interest, the good tree of *sensibilité* produces fruits by which it may instantly be known.

The centrality of *sensibilité* in Mlle de Scudéry's vision of things is perhaps best demonstrated by the relationship which exists between *tendresse*, the derivative of *sensibilité*, and certain of the most prominent features of the landscape which Mlle de Scudéry creates in her work. One of the most obvious of these features is that Mlle de Scudéry's lovers - at least those lovers who appear to be offered for the reader to admire - display a *respect* and *soumission* to their mistress which is often taken to inordinate lengths. Diametrically opposed to these respectful and submissive lovers is another group, comprising lovers who consider their mistress simply as an instrument of their own gratification and who lack the hero's ability to put her feelings and wishes before their own. One of the details of *Le Grand Cyrus* which most called forth the scorn of Mlle de Scudéry's detractors was the frequency with which the heroine, Mandane, is abducted by *infâmes ravisseurs* - none of whom, however, carries his infamy to the point of subjecting Mandane to the ultimate indignity.[8] Such abductors merely represent the extreme form of a more generalized tendency, the possessiveness which, in the absence of *tendresse*, is the inevitable concomitant of love and leads the suitor to assert his rights over those of the woman. By contrast, heroic lovers tend to refuse to make any kind of demands of the woman; they are reluctant to do or say anything that might imply that they have any kind of rights over her or she any obligation to them. It is for this reason that heroic lovers typically are the complete reverse of assertive, preferring when circumstances permit to suffer in silence rather than declare themselves, asking nothing in return for their love: Aronce wishes for Clélie's friendship only, whereas Horace seeks to press forward to the *Terres Inconnues*. Nowhere is the contrast between submissive and possessive lovers more clearly brought out than when, as occasionally happens, a character passes from one group to the other. There is for example the case of Mazare, one of Mandane's abductors, who undergoes a kind of conversion, repenting of his past misdeeds and resolving to live differently in the future. 'Iusques icy', he exclaims, 'i'auois aimé Mandane pour l'amour de moy: mais ie veux commencer de l'aimer pour l'amour d'elle seule. Ie ne sçay pas ... si ie la pourray aimer sans desirs: mais ie sçay du moins que ie l'aimeray sans esperance' (*Cyrus*, V, 439). One of the first signs of his change of attitude is his attempt to persuade the Roy de Pont, another of Mandane's abductors, to give her up. 'I'aime Mandane plus parfaitement que vous', he rebukes his rival, 'puisque ne pouuant en estre aimé, ie sçay borner mes esperances, & ne chercher plus que son repos. Si vous sçauiez, adiousta t'il, aussi bien aimer que ie le sçay, vous sentiriez plus que vous ne faites, les souffrances de la personne aimée' (*Cyrus*, V, 455f). What has happened is that *tendresse* has suddenly invaded love, reversing its downward pull; Mazare has been touched by Mandane's sufferings to the point of vicariously experiencing them, and this has led him to subordinate his own personal interests and wishes to hers. Once again, *tendresse* is seen both as the antidote to self-interest and as the only alternative to it.

In this scheme of things, in which the lover demonstrates his *tendresse* by his deference to his mistress, a particular problem is posed by jealousy. It is safe to say that of all the many subjects discussed by Mlle de Scudéry's characters, jealousy is probably the most frequent, though no definitive conclusion is ever reached. The difficulty is that jealousy would seem to be an infringement of the ideal of *tendresse*, an instance of possessiveness, implying that the jealous partner has some kind of proprietorial rights over the other. Yet at the same time, absence of jealousy suggests both that the lover is unduly sure of himself (an immodesty which carries with it the suspicion that self-interest has not been completely eradicated from his motivation) and that his feelings are not so intense as they might be. Some indication of the range and diversity of possible attitudes to jealousy is given by a curious episode which occurs towards the end of *Le Grand Cyrus* and which is entitled 'Le Banquet des sept sages'. Among the points put forward in the debate are that jealousy increases love, provided there is no foundation for it; that it always accompanies love, but is inconsistent with it; that a lover should be capable of jealousy without ever being jealous; that if jealousy is unjustified in a given situation, one ought not to have it, and if it is justified, one ought not to love the person who occasioned it; that love without jealousy is 'trop tiede'; that jealousy is justified because it is impossible to love anything without being afraid to lose that thing (*Cyrus*, IX, 466). Like the sharp contrast which exists between submissive and possessive lovers, the inconclusiveness of the jealousy debate and its frequent recurrence in Mlle de Scudéry's work underline the central position which the concept of *tendresse* occupies in her thought; jealousy is an insoluble problem precisely because its presence and its absence can alike be construed as a lack of *tendresse*.

Mlle de Scudéry's fear of the possessiveness to which love is prone, which nevertheless must be avoided if love is to be authentic and lasting, leads her to express serious reservations about the institution of marriage. The reason for this less than enthusiastic attitude to marriage is partly of course the obvious one - that whereas a suitor may be expected to submit himself totally to the wishes of the woman, the same is not true of a husband, who through marriage is given rights over his wife and can legitimately make demands of her. In the 'Histoire de Sapho', Mlle de Scudéry makes Sapho a mouthpiece for the view that marriage is 'vn long esclauage' which she (Sapho) intends to avoid: 'ie ne me resoudrois iamais à faire de mon Esclaue mon Tiran' (*Cyrus*, X, 345). But there is more to Mlle de Scudéry's anti-marriage stance than this. The desire to marry, she believes, is a sign of self-interest on the part of the lover, because it signifies that love, instead of being an end in itself, is merely a means to an end, and that the lover is striving towards a goal from which he will derive some kind of personal benefit. Sapho directly challenges the traditional view that it is marriage which legitimizes love: 'ie ne suis nullement dans le sentiment de ceux qui parlent de l'amour, comme d'vne chose qui ne peut estre innocente, si l'on n'a le dessein de s'espouser'. On the contrary, she argues, a desire to marry positively invalidates love: 'ie veux bien qu'on espere d'estre aimé ... mais ie ne veux pas qu'on espere rien dauantage'. The reason for this reversal of a commonly held principle is that marriage involves a commitment to love another for the rest of one's life. Yet for love to last, it has to possess a *tendresse* which is incompatible with the slightest taint of self-interest, and the desire to marry is just such a taint. Hence, in marriage, it is inevitable for the partners to 'passer bientost de l'amour à l'indifference, & de l'indifference à la haine & au mespris' (*Cyrus*, X, 414f). Marriage is to be avoided because it is not consistent with *tendresse*, *tendresse* being the only way to achieve the permanence of a relationship which marriage seeks to guarantee.

Mlle de Scudéry's determination to track down and eradicate even the smallest traces of self-interest in love is such that it affects her whole conception of what love is. Again and again, she insists that love has nothing to do with reason, that it is an affair of the heart and not of the head, that the lover has no choice in the matter of whether to fall in love or not. Whatever the similarities between *amitié* and *amour*, the essential difference, as Aronce makes clear in the *tendresse* discussion, is that whereas *amitié* is compatible with the exercise of the judgment and the will, *amour* is not, being a force which as it were takes control of the lover from the outside, a state which cannot be voluntarily entered into or ended. It is Mlle de Scudéry's rigorous pursuit of self-interest which explains this emphasis - a constant one in her work - on the irrational nature of love. If the lover is able to give a reason for his love (the woman's beauty, say, or his gratitude to the woman for what she has done for him), this implies that he loves the woman not for what she is in herself but for what she has done for him, that he is concerned with what he can derive from the relationship rather than what he can give to it. In the 'Histoire de Sapho', Phaon lists the causes of his love for Sapho, including a reference to gratitude, and this incurs Sapho's displeasure: 'si l'on ne m'aimoit que parce que i'aimerois, on me feroit vn outrage tres sensible'. Gratitude, she objects, may give rise to *amitié*, but not to *amour*. 'Jugez donc, Phaon', she concludes, 'si ie trouuerois bon que vous pussiez m'aimer par nulle autre raison que parce que vous me trouuez aimable, & parce que vous ne pouuez vous empescher d'auoir de l'affection pour moy' (*Cyrus*, X, 560f). The guarantee that the lover is free from self-interest is thus not only the form in which his love expresses itself (his total submission to the woman's wishes) but also the way in which his love comes into being; the ideal is to be unable to account for one's love, to have no explanation of love other than that one cannot help it. Another story from *Le Grand Cyrus* is that of Parthenie, who after a first unhappy experience of marriage vows that if ever she marries again, it will only be when she is convinced that her lover is not in any way influenced by her beauty; she lays down the principle that 'quiconque n'aimera que la beauté de Parthenie, n'acquerra iamais son amitié', because, as she puts it, 'ie veux qu'on aime Parthenie toute entiere' (*Cyrus*, VI, 110). Nor is this stance dictated, as might be imagined, merely by the wish to achieve a relationship founded on something more than simple physical desire. The point emerges from a conversation later in the story in which Parthenie explains that her reason for setting her face against an affection 'fondée sur des choses passageres comme la beauté & la richesse' is that such a love would be at the mercy of time and of the vicissitudes of life. *Amour-tendresse* (although she does not use the term) is clearly the ideal towards which she is striving:

> Je veux donc qu'on m'aime seulement par inclination, & par la connoissance de mon ame, de mon esprit, & de mon humeur. De plus, ie veux qu'on me puisse aimer laide & pauure si ie la suis, ou si ie la deuiens: & ie veux enfin qu'on n'aime que moy: qu'on m'aime ardemment; qu'on m'aime tousiours; qu'on ne face que ce que ie veux; qu'on ne desire que ce qui me plaist; & qu'on m'obeïsse aueuglément & sans repugnance (*Cyrus*, VI, 202).

Parthenie's beauty is not the 'real' Parthenie any more than her riches are; she wishes to be loved for what she is in herself rather than for what she has. Her views on love demonstrate the close link which exists between the ideal of total obedience and that of being unable to account for the origins of love; both are signs of love's disinterestedness and hence of its permanence, and both are aspects of the same recognition of the woman not as a possession but as a person in her own right. Like love, which must be freed from the ulterior motive represented by marriage, the woman is to be regarded as an end in herself.

For Mlle de Scudéry, then, love must involve only the heart and not the head, since otherwise it will inevitably be associated with the calculation of benefit, and hence with self-interest. Parthenie's rejection of all forms of love other than those founded on *inclination* rules out both *Tendre-sur-Estime* and *Tendre-sur-Reconnaissance* as suitable goals for the lover. Such destinations may be appropriate in *amitié*, but lovers must make for *Tendre-sur-Inclination*. The vital importance of *inclination* in love is stressed again in one of Mlle de Scudéry's later works by a character who shares Parthenie's belief that 'il n'y a que l'amour qui naist par inclination que ie puisse appeler amour', adding that 'pour bien aimer il ne faut point sçauoir pourquoy on aime, il ne faut point dire i'aime, par ce que ie suis aimé, par ce que i'ay de l'obligation, par ce que i'ay de l'estime, mais seulement i'ayme par ce que i'ayme; par ce que i'y suis forcé, & que ie ne m'en puis empescher'.[9] Again, the operation of *inclination* is seen in the lover's inability to give any adequate explanation of why he is in love or to control the mysterious force which has seized him. This force is felt to be as strange and immediate in its effect as a phenomenon which occurs in the natural sphere, that of magnetism. In the course of one of the discussions in *Le Grand Cyrus*, love is likened to the natural 'simpathie' by which the magnet attracts iron and which cannot be destroyed, although its effect may be temporarily impeded; for this reason, it is argued, it is impossible to fall in love with a woman for a second time after having effectively ceased to love her (*Cyrus*, IX, 462f). The irrationality of love thus plays a twofold role in Mlle de Scudéry's thinking. On the one hand, since irrationality is the essence of love, there is, as we have seen, a natural assocation of love with disorder - an assocation which can only be broken by the presence of *tendresse*. On the other hand, the irrationality of love – in the sense that love's origins cannot be explained – is also a way of guaranteeing that *tendresse* is present, complementing as it does the lover's submission and obedience. The paradox is more apparent than real; it is simply that the heart is the sphere in which both basic tendencies attributed to human behaviour, self-assertion and self-forgetfulness, can be seen to operate. One of these tendencies explains the need for *tendresse*; the other allows it to come into existence.

In love, then, *inclination*, the strange magnetism which draws a man and a woman together for no other discernible reason than that they are what they are, is necessary because only *inclination* works independently of the mind and will; it cannot therefore be associated with any ulterior motive, and *amour d'inclination* must of necessity be *amour-tendresse*. This emphasis on *inclination* has its practical outworking in the techniques which Mlle de Scudéry chooses in order to convey to the reader the workings of her characters' minds. Along with the submissiveness of the lover and the inexplicableness of love, the other striking feature of Mlle de Scudéry's analysis of love is her fondness for showing a *surprise de l'amour*: that is, the lover is initially not aware that he is in love, but attributes the new emotions he experiences to other causes. In other words, the lover is at first unable to identify his love correctly, erroneously labelling it (most commonly) pity or esteem or gratitude or *amitié*. As love progresses, the lover will at some stage have a flash of insight in which he realizes that he has misunderstood himself, and that he has been in love all the time. The progress to lucidity is not always recounted in detail; on many occasions, Mlle de Scudéry is content simply to state that the moment of insight arrives, without concerning herself too much with what prepared it. When the progress to lucidity is described, however, what usually happens is that the lover encounters new experiences which become increasingly difficult to pigeonhole under pity or esteem or whatever category he has chosen; there is a period of confusion in which the character's self-understanding is subjected to

increasing pressure until the moment when the scales fall from his
eyes and when, to quote Mandane, describing her own experience,
'en vn moment i'ay veû cent choses que ie n'auois point veuës: ou
pour mieux dire, ie les ay veuës d'vne autre façon, que ie ne les
voyois pas auparauant' (*Cyrus*, II, 24). Love enters the fortress
by stealth and is only recognized when it is too strong to be
easily dislodged; it first shows its presence by influencing
behaviour subliminally, and there is some delay before the
conscious mind wakes to the reality of the situation.

Mlle de Scudéry of course does not always use the *surprise de
l'amour*; there are many stories within the pages of *Le Grand Cyrus*
and *Clélie* in which it does not occur. Yet it is frequent enough
in Mlle de Scudéry's work to be felt as some kind of norm. The
fact that in *Clélie* a *surprise de l'amour* does not happen for
Aronce is clearly regarded by Mlle de Scudéry as a breach of faith
with her readers, calling for some explanation: 'ce qu'il y eut
d'estrange dans son amour', she says of Aronce, 'fut qu'il
n'ignora pas vn moment, la nature de l'affection qu'il auoit pour
elle [Clélie], comme font pour l'ordinaire ceux qui n'ont iamais
eu de passion' (*Clélie*, I, 192). Inability to identify love
correctly is not, however, confined to the complete novice in
love, but is widespread enough to be viewed as one of the accepted
conventions of romance. In a satirical work which pokes fun at
romance commonplaces, Bougeant, an eighteenth-century detractor of
romances in general and Mlle de Scudéry in particular, lists the
*surprise de l'amour* among the 'trente-six formalités' which, in
the romance world, must precede marriage. The first of these
formalities, says the character who is obviously Bougeant's
mouthpiece, is to fall in love. 'Or cela est fort plaisant', he
continues, 'car on l'est quelquefois une année entière sans le
savoir, & il y en a tel qui ne s'en doute seulement pas. S'il a
arrêté ses regards sur une personne, c'est sans dessein: s'il l'a
trouvée extrêmement aimable, ses sentimens se sont bornés à
l'estime & à l'admiration; tout au plus il croit n'avoir pour elle
que de l'amitié'. The lover who is surprised in this way begins
to wonder why his sleep is disturbed, why he has lost his

'enjouement ordinaire' and become 'distrait & mélancolique', and it is this awareness of a change which precipitates the knowledge that he is in love.[10] The fact that Bougeant's work is dated 1735 is a pointer both to the lasting influence of the romances of the seventeenth century and to the way in which the spirit of these romances is felt to be contained in certain characteristic features. It is clear that one of these features is the *surprise de l'amour*; the traveller in what Bougeant calls the *pays de Romancie* is bound to see it and needs to have it commented on.

Commonplace as it is, the *surprise de l'amour* in Mlle de Scudéry's work acquires a particular significance from being set alongside her emphasis on the importance of *inclination*. The fact that love typically comes as a surprise is an indication that *inclination* is at work; far from being able to account for his love, the lover does not even recognize its presence. The *surprise de l'amour* is consistent with the idea of love as a force which comes from outside the lover and takes control of his actions, forcing him to do and say things which do not represent conscious decisions on his part. Consequently, there can by definition be no ulterior motive, no calculation of reward or benefit, and hence no self-interest. Although the *surprise de l'amour* does not guarantee *tendresse* (possessive lovers too may initially fail to recognize that they are in love) it can nevertheless be a promise of *tendresse* and all its benefits – the permanence, the authenticity, the heights of emotional experience which intimate communion affords. Another way in which the *surprise de l'amour* confers a heightened value on love is that a falling in love experienced as a surprise represents a decisive break with the past. The lover finds that his old familiar ways of making sense of his experience no longer suffice; love is a surprise not only in the sense that it implants itself by stealth, but also in the sense that it is accompanied by astonishment and wonder. For the surprised lover, the act of falling in love is the equivalent of an initiation into a new dimension of existence not previously accessible, an initiation for which the discovery of *Terres Inconnues* is a highly appropriate figure. In the case of the woman, this discovery is of special significance. Typically, Mlle de Scudéry's heroines have a particular awareness of the disorders which love can cause, and therefore believe that to be in love is not consistent with the very highest standards of feminine virtue, those which they have elected to follow. If they were conscious from the beginning of being in love, they would make a determined effort to eradicate their passion from their heart. As it is, however, they cannot take steps to banish love until they have realized that it is present, by which time love has become too firmly entrenched to be removed. The fact that love comes as a surprise leaves room for the operation not only of *tendresse* but also of the moral and intellectual qualities which, as we have seen, provide the soil for *tendresse* to flourish in. Through the *surprise de l'amour*, it is possible to portray female characters who are paragons of virtue but who nevertheless fall in love; what has happened to them is not within their own control.

It may be said then that the prevalence of the *surprise de l'amour* in Mlle de Scudéry's work is explicable in terms of the importance she attaches to *tendresse*, that it is part of the same relentless attack on self-interest and of her repeated insistence that love is only worthy of the name if the lover cannot give reasons for it. At the same time, however, the *surprise de l'amour* impinges on Mlle de Scudéry's concept of *tendresse* in another way also. As has already been pointed out, love surprises the lover by assuming one of a number of disguises, the most common of which are pity, esteem, gratitude and *amitié*. What allows love to assume these various disguises is that all of them are different avatars of the spirit of *tendresse* which for Mlle de Scudéry is to be a feature of love too. The basic confusion arises over *amour* and *amitié*, and over the requirement that *tendresse* be present in both. If *tendresse* exists in a relationship between people of different sexes, it is difficult – not least for the participants – to decide whether it is as part of love or friendship; in the words of one character from *Clélie*, 'les sentimens qu'vne amour vertueuse inspire, ressemblent si fort à ceux qu'vne tendre amitié donne, que quand on veut s'y tromper

on s'y trompe' (*Clélie*, VI, 997). To put it another way, the
ideal of love as *amour-tendresse* demands that all that is highest
and noblest in friendship should be present in love also. 'Pour
former vne amour que la fortune & le temps ne puissent faire
changer', writes Mlle de Scudéry late in life, 'il faut que toutes
les grandes qualitez qui font naistre & qui entretiennent les
grandes amitiez s'y rencontrent';[11] in view of this, the ambiguity
which can arise over whether a given state is *amitié* or *amour* is
hardly surprising. The possibility of confusion is compounded by
the lover's respect for the woman, which can, as the case of
Aronce has already shown, lead him to hope for nothing in return
for his love other than friendship from her; 'la plus indubitable
marque d'vne grande passion', according to another character in
*Clélie*, 'est de voir vn Amant qui malgré tous ses suplices, reçoit
auec plaisir le plus petit tesmoignage d'amitié que sa Maistresse
luy puisse donner' (*Clélie*, VI, 979). Add to this the fact that a
given relationship may start off as *amitié* and progress to *amour* -
that is, that a man and a woman, having arrived together at
*Tendre*, do not stop there, but journey on to the *Terres Inconnues*
- and it will be seen that *tendre amitié* and *amour*, different
though they may be in their essence, are similar enough in form to
be easily mistaken for each other. As for the other common
disguises of love - gratitude, esteem and pity - it is because
they too, like love, partake of *tendresse*, that cases of mistaken
identity may occur. On the *Carte de Tendre*, the traveller has not
one, but three possible destinations, each of them a part of what
is essentially the same whole; beside *Tendre-sur-Inclination* lie
both *Tendre-sur- Reconnoissance* and *Tendre-sur-Estime*. There is
no *Tendre-sur-Compassion*, but that is simply because suffering
with another is not a route to *tendresse*, but a definition of it.
Love's tendency to assume the disguises which it most commonly
chooses is thus largely explicable in terms of the topography of
the *pays de Tendre*; the *surprise de l'amour* is a commonplace in
Mlle de Scudéry's work because *Tendre-sur-Inclination* may be
approached either from *amitié* or *amour*, and because *Tendre* itself
may be approached by different routes. In other words, there are

different manifestations of the same basic willingness to identify with the other, to seek the other's good and the other's happiness; love is only one of these manifestations, and it is easy to be misled by the general family resemblance.

These then are the prominent features of the Scudéry landscape which can be related back to the concept of *tendresse* - the lover's total submissiveness and refusal to make demands of the woman, the sharp contrast between submissive and possessive lovers, the value attached to love as opposed to marriage, the inexplicable nature of love and the demonstration of this in the *surprise de l'amour*. Each of these features reflects the same urge to proscribe self-interest and to replace it with the self-effacing identification which *tendresse* always involves. Self-interest and its opposite are of course preoccupations not only of Mlle de Scudéry, but of her age in general. In her work, however, these preoccupations are the vehicle for a particular brand of feminism. Behind her emphasis on *tendresse* lies a desire to revalue the role of women, to create a framework for relationships in which women will be treated not as objects but as subjects, not as possessions but as individuals in their own right. Mlle de Scudéry is concerned not so much with male relationships, as with relationships which women have, both with each other and with the opposite sex. In whichever of these a woman is involved, *tendresse* guarantees that her own inner subjective world will be recognized and respected by the partner and that if the woman's interests are to be subordinated to the partner's, it will not be compulsorily but as the result of a free act of choice. In *tendresse*, two free, autonomous beings approach each other and recognize the selfhood of the other by treating the other as the self. To liberty therefore is joined a kind of equality; the ideal is a situation in which each partner alike both gives and receives. It may seem strange to talk of equality when in a relationship the man is expected to submit himself totally to the woman's wishes. Clearly Mlle de Scudéry feels that normally both male autonomy and female dependence can be taken for granted, and that it is female autonomy that needs to be asserted.

The man's submissiveness to the woman constitutes no threat to his sense of himself as a separate, unique individual, but simply an acknowledgement that the woman too is as he is. When this acknowledgement is made, there is a sense in which the man and the woman are equals; it is this equality which makes it possible to realize the ideal of communion and sharing. Liberty, equality and fraternity are all simply aspects of the same reality, and are all claimed for women in relationships both with each other and with the opposite sex.

This whole complex of themes and preoccupations, and the concept of *tendresse* which pervades them all, provides a backcloth against which the *Carte de Tendre* can be more clearly seen for what it is. It goes without saying that the *Carte de Tendre* is a pictorial representation of the thinking on *tendresse* which articulates itself both in the discussion between Aronce and Clélie and elsewhere in Mlle de Scudéry's work. It is time, therefore, to return to the *Carte de Tendre* itself, in order to see how far Mlle de Scudéry's views on *tendresse* illuminate and explain the actual details of the map, the circumstances surrounding its composition, and the reactions of contemporaries to it.

CONCLUSION

THE *CARTE DE TENDRE* REVISITED

Like the *tendresse* discussion between Aronce and Clélie, the *Carte de Tendre* is a summary, a small-scale version of an insight which is developed through Mlle de Scudéry's work as a whole. To arrive at *Tendre* is to reach the destination which Mlle de Scudéry sets as the goal of relationships in general, the intimacy and identification which depends so heavily on *sensibilité*. The speediest of the routes from the town of *Nouvelle-Amitié* to *Tendre*, that by the river of *Inclination*, represents the immediate affinity which can spring up between two kindred spirits, whether of the same sex or not; this route, while only one of three alternatives in friendship, is more or less obligatory for lovers. Of the other two routes, the one which most betrays its link with *sensibilité* is that which finishes at *Tendre-sur-Reconnoissance*. The traveller on this road progresses through *étapes* which all represent different aspects of his general desire to seek not his own happiness but that of his partner - *Complaisance*, *Soumission* and *Petits-Soins*, this last reminding him not to neglect small and seemingly insignificant details - to *Assiduité* and *Empressement*, expressions of the constancy of his attitude and his readiness to act on the other's behalf; his giving of himself to the other is not grudging, but something in which he delights. All the qualities represented by these halting-places would seem to be summed up in the next two which are reached, *Sensibilité* and *Tendresse*, and these lead (after a further reminder of the importance of *Obéissance*) to *Constante-Amitié* and hence to *Tendre-sur-*

*Reconnoissance*. The seeming strangeness of having to pass through *Tendresse* before arriving at *Tendre-sur-Reconnoissance* is accounted for by the fact that, as Clélie makes clear in the discussion with Aronce, gratitude is typically a response to an act which demonstrates *tendresse*; *Tendre-sur-Reconnoissance* stands for the situation in which each partner, out of gratitude for the consideration shown him, replies in kind. Another interesting feature of this particular route is that the traveller who goes astray risks falling into the *Mer d'Inimitié*, reached by way of *Indiscretion*, *Perfidie*, *Médisance* and *Meschanceté*. Significantly, these places are clustered around *Orgueil*, which, being perched high upon a rock, overlooks and dominates them all; the suggestion is obviously that these defects have pride as their root cause. Of all the routes to *Tendre*, it is that to *Tendre-sur-Reconnoissance* which demonstrates not only the importance which Mlle de Scudéry attributes to *sensibilité* in the generation of *tendresse*, but also her tendency to view *tendresse* and self-interest as positive and negative poles of human behaviour.

The remaining route on the *Carte de Tendre* - that which finishes at *Tendre-sur-Estime* - is less obviously related to *sensibilité*. It remains true, however, that the same thread of consideration for the feelings and wishes of the other runs through all the qualities encountered on this route. These qualities divide fairly obviously into two groups. Those encountered early on the journey (*Iolis Vers*, *Billet galant*, *Billet doux*) continue the thought behind the naming of the first halting place, *Grand esprit*, and the second group consists of those which belong more properly to *Grand Coeur* (*Probité*, *Generosité*, *Exactitude*, *Respect* and *Bonté*); *Sincerité* is placed between the two groups perhaps to indicate that though a moral quality it is also an intellectual one, expressing itself in the verses and letters which a *Grand esprit* composes. The purpose of such productions is of course to compliment and pay tribute to the partner in the relationship, thus enhancing his sense of his own worth. After *Grand Coeur*, the names of the *étapes* stress the traveller's strict attention to what is required of him (*Probité*,

*Exactitude*), his readiness to serve the other's interests
(*Generosité*, *Bonté*), and once again his refusal to make demands of
the other (*Respect*). The qualities which give rise to esteem are
in no case individual virtues or gifts of mind, but rather pat-
terns of behaviour which the individual displays in his relationships with others. The esteem which their presence evokes is not
a distant, objective appraisal, but rather the verdict of someone
who is closely involved with the possessor and who benefits
directly from the qualities in question. The *Grand Coeur* is in
reality no different from the *âme sensible*; it is simply that the
basic attitude towards others which he represents is being seen in
more specifically moral terms, considered in respect of the way in
which this basic attitude works itself out in the creation of
character. Whether character of this kind is, as Clélie believes,
the necessary precondition for *sensibilité*, or whether, as Aronce
argues, it is *sensibilité* which is the necessary precondition for
character, the relationship between the intellectual and moral
qualities associated with the road to *Tendre-sur-Estime* and the
qualities of the heart associated with the road to *Tendre-sur-
Reconnoissance* is closer than might appear from a superficial
glance at the map.

There are of course limits to the accuracy and completeness
with which any allegory can reflect the objective reality to which
it relates; the highlighting of certain aspects of this reality
inevitably means that others are left in the shade. The *Carte de
Tendre* is no exception to this general rule. The symbolism of the
map - in particular that of the routes to *Tendre-sur-
Reconnoissance* and to *Tendre-sur-Estime*, with their journeys
through various *étapes* - is a highly appropriate method of
underlining the progressive nature of the journey into friendship
and the need for a certain amount of time to elapse before *Tendre*
is reached. Similarly, the risks involved in the journey - the
*Mer d'Inimitié* and the *Lac d'Indiference* will claim a certain
percentage of travellers - effectively suggest that *tendre amitié*
requires some kind of initiation and trial, such as the period of
waiting imposed on Pellisson. What the symbolism of the *étapes*

does less well is to convey the idea that the journey is not only progressive but cumulative. As we have seen, it needs Celere, in *Clélie*, to point out that although the traveller progresses from one stage to the next in his journey through the *pays de Tendre*, in friendship one cannot afford to leave any of these qualities behind; though the map does not really indicate this, both *Tendre-sur-Reconnoissance* and *Tendre-sur-Estime* are not only destinations, but summaries of all that has gone before. Moreover, if the friend is to accumulate all the qualities represented by the *étapes* on any given route, ideal friendship is achieved not simply by choosing one of the routes but by travelling by all three simultaneously; in other words, friendship does not consist merely of *Reconnoissance* or *Inclination* or *Estime*, but of all three together. The deficiency of the map in this respect is made clear in one of Mlle de Scudéry's late works, the *Conversations morales* of 1686. In a discussion specifically devoted to the *Carte de Tendre*, Mlle de Scudéry reiterates her conviction that 'la marque de l'amitié parfaite ... est la communauté de toutes sortes de biens sans exception'. Given this definition, all three routes of the *Carte de Tendre* must be taken, 'car pour former une amitié parfaite & constante, il faut que les deux personnes qui s'aiment ayent de la simpathie ensemble, qu'elles ayent de l'estime, & même de l'admiration l'une pour l'autre, qu'elles ayent le coeur noble, tendre & bien-fait pour sentir les bons offices & pour les rendre'.[1] With its symbolism of a journey involving choice of route and progression towards a destination, the *Carte de Tendre* cannot do full justice to the need for all the qualities in question to be present in friendship at the same time, though it goes some way towards meeting this objection by presenting *Reconnoissance*, *Estime* and *Inclination* as being at once different and the same, linked by the presence of the word *Tendre* in their title.

A more important respect in which the *Carte de Tendre* fails to reflect Mlle de Scudéry's thought with complete accuracy is in what it has to say about the relationship between *amitié* and *amour*. As we have seen, the *pays de Tendre* is not the same as the *pays d'amour*; Mlle de Scudéry herself constantly underlines the difference, which is further illustrated by the fact that in the Scudéry milieu, travellers to *Tendre* include not only men but other women also. Yet as the discussion between Aronce and Clélie shows, *tendresse* is the overriding aim of love as well as of friendship. Again, the *Carte de Tendre*'s representation of experience as a journey has both strengths and weaknesses when it comes to portraying the relationship which for Mlle de Scudéry exists between *tendresse*, *amitié* and *amour*. The map well brings out the ambivalent status of *Tendre*, which may be either simply a stage on the longer journey to the *Terres Inconnues* or a final destination in its own right, a place where, as Zumthor perceptively remarks, 'l'on jette l'ancre' and which consequently suggests 'une stabilité imposée soudain au-dessus d'un flot toujours fuyant'.[2] The *pays de Tendre*, which is surrounded on three sides by dangerous waters, is a little enclave of permanence and solidity in a world which is inimical to both - a vision which is entirely in accord with Mlle de Scudéry's account of how *tendresse* functions in a relationship. Similarly, the fact that the traveller may stop short at *Tendre* is the pictorial equivalent of her belief that in certain circumstances at least, *tendre amitié* can provide an acceptable substitute for love. The fact that the *pays de Tendre* can either be seen as complete in itself or as opening out on to the *Terres Inconnues* adjacent to it, is Mlle de Scudéry's way of conveying what, as we have seen, is a constant in her thinking - that *tendresse*, though it may be close to love in some ways, is not synonymous with it. Again, however, the journey symbolism is less successful in suggesting the need for the traveller to accumulate qualities; just as he must leave nothing behind him in his journey to *Tendre*, so too, if he launches out into the *Mer Dangereuse*, he must carry with him all that his travels through the *pays de Tendre* have brought him. In other words, the map suggests that *tendre amitié*, rather than being an essential component of love, as Mlle de Scudéry believes it to be, is instead a preliminary to it. The fact is, of course, that although one may stop at *Tendre*, there is no need to go through *tendre amitié* before falling in love. Although the *Carte de Tendre* does not show this, Mlle de Scudéry conceives of *Tendre-sur-Inclination* as common to both *amitié* and *amour*, and it is this dual nationality, so to speak, which can deceive the lover into misinterpreting his state as one of the various forms of *tendresse*. In order to reproduce the range of Mlle de Scudéry's thinking on *tendresse*, the *Carte de Tendre* would thus have to be amended to show *Tendre-sur-Inclination* as a kind of no man's land, the *pays de Tendre* and the *Terres Inconnues* as united in a federation, and the features of the two countries so similar that it is possible for the traveller to be unsure which of them he is in.

In view of the *Carte de Tendre*'s inability to represent in full what *tendresse* means for Mlle de Scudéry, it is hardly surprising that it should have been misunderstood by some at least of her contemporaries. It appears to have been Mlle de Scudéry's fate to have been in her lifetime a trendsetter whose ideas, in the process of being transmitted to a wider public, were inevitably subject to distortion and misunderstanding. To say, as she does, that *tendresse* is common to *amitié* and *amour*, that love may be wrongly identified as *tendre amitié*, is to risk providing a convenient cover for relationships for which neither *tendresse* nor *amitié* would be appropriate terms. In a sense, then, the criticisms levelled at the *Carte de Tendre* by Boileau and Arnauld are justified; the proximity of the *pays de Tendre* and the *pays d'amour* can be used to facilitate access to the latter. Yet it is clear that far from encouraging contemporary *galanterie*, Mlle de Scudéry's intention is precisely to remedy its deficiencies and to set it on a higher plane altogether. The safeguards she seeks are not to restrict and control relationships, but to transform them from within. She is a champion of freedom, particularly for the woman, but it is freedom shorn of the risks of disorder, since it is freedom to do not as one likes but as the other wishes. Whatever may have been its effect on social attitudes, the *Carte de Tendre* is meant not as a charter for licence or as a

justification for things as they are; it is rather the record of a
vision of things as they might be.

If this distance between the ideal expressed by the *Carte de
Tendre* and commonly observed social reality serves to explain the
stance of the major seventeenth-century critics of Mlle de Scudéry
- criticism of the *Carte de Tendre* coupled with admiration of her
- it also throws light on the place occupied by the *Carte de
Tendre* among other allegorical maps of the same period. As we
have seen, the *Carte de Tendre* has been felt to be more akin to
the long-standing tradition of spiritual allegory than to most
contemporary productions which, like d'Aubignac's map, seek to
chart the *Royaume de Coquetterie*.[3] The reasons for this family
likeness can be traced back to Mlle de Scudéry's concept of
*tendresse*, which the *Carte de Tendre* in its own way embodies.
There are some striking affinities between this concept and ideas
which in Mlle de Scudéry's time are common in the religious and
moral sphere. By the middle of the seventeenth century it is part
of accepted wisdom to make a distinction between two kinds of
love, one which seeks the good of the beloved, the other which
seeks the beloved as an object of possession. Speaking of love
for God, for instance, Saint François de Sales distinguishes
between what he calls *amour de bienveillance* and *amour de
convoitise*; the former is the higher form, manifesting itself when
'nous aimons Dieu pour l'amour de lui-même' rather than for
anything that God may do for us.[4] For Descartes, the terminology
is slightly different but the distinction remains the same, and
applies not simply to spiritual love but to love in general. 'On
distingue communement deux sortes d'Amour', he writes, 'l'une
desquelles est nommée Amour de bienvueillance, c'est à dire, qui
incite à vouloir du bien à ce qu'on aime; l'autre est nommée Amour
de concupiscence, c'est à dire, qui fait désirer la chose qu'on
aime'.[5] *Amour de concupiscence* is thus simply a form of self-love,
contrasted with the unselfishness of *amour de bienveillance*. Put
in those terms, the doctrine of two loves is the restatement of a
principle adopted by theologians from Saint Augustine onwards, a
principle which states that all human behaviour is ultimately

traceable to one of two motives, love of self or love of God. Saint Augustine represents these two primary motives by two cities, Babylon and Jerusalem. An equally well known simile is that of Raymond Sebond, who pictures the existence, in the soul, of 'un arbre d'amour', rooted in either 'amour de soy' or 'amour de Dieu'. The value of human affections depends on which of these constitutes the root of the tree; the former can give rise only to vice, whereas the latter produces good fruit.[6] Whether an action is to be classed as virtuous or not depends not on its external form but on which bias of soul it illustrates and springs from.

For all the apparent distance between them, it is perhaps alongside such allegorical representations of human behaviour that the *Carte de Tendre* may most appropriately be ranged. It goes without saying of course that Mlle de Scudéry is not a theologian, and that specifically religious questions, though not absent from her work, are not one of her main concerns. Yet in her account of *tendresse* the ideas of the theologians appear in another guise. In the *pays de Tendre* too one may travel under the pull of two different influences; on the one hand, *Tendre* beckons, but on the other there is *Orgueil*, luring the traveller eventually to his doom in the *Mer d'Inimitié*. Like the roots of Raymond Sebond's tree, these two influences are mutually exclusive - one may follow one or the other but not both at the same time - and determine the moral value to be attached to actions which derive from them. Consistently Mlle de Scudéry associates *tendresse* with goodness, seeing its presence as legitimizing a relationship and giving it the power to become ennobling instead of degrading. Although no preacher, the reaction she is seeking from her readers is a kind of conversion experience, a turning away from the self-centredness of *amour de concupiscence* to the gift of self involved in *amour de bienveillance*. Mlle de Scudéry's diagnosis of human behaviour is in essence very similar to that of the theologians; the root cause of evil and suffering in the world is love of self, and the remedy is to replace it with what may be regarded as the secular counterpart of love of God, namely disinterested love of another. In other words, salvation consists for Mlle de Scudéry in treating one's fellows as the believer treats God; *tendre amitié* is a union which is almost mystical in quality since, like mystical union of the believer with God, *tendresse* involves becoming one with the other while still, paradoxically, remaining oneself. It is of course particularly the woman in a relationship who replaces God as a recipient for love of this kind; Mlle de Scudéry's feminism, her assertion of the value of woman, takes the form of a desire to divinize her sex, a conviction that women, like God, should be loved for what they are in themselves rather than for what they possess or for what they can give to the lover.

One may say then that while the point of contact between Mlle de Scudéry and contemporary *galanterie* is her feminism, her support for the freedom of the woman, she also relates to moral and religious thinking of the time through her preoccupation with self-interest and with *tendresse* as an antidote to it. The importance of Mlle de Scudéry's contribution to the debate on such issues lies in the *sensibilité* which is central to her vision, the place which she gives to feeling as a means of relating both to the external world and to other people. It is this *sensibilité* which makes it possible to approach another person with *amour de bienveillance* instead of *amour de concupiscence*, to respect their individuality and experience their inner life vicariously. Self-interest is the fatal flaw which makes relationships subject to the ravages of time and which encourages sham and deceit; *sensibilité*, which neutralizes the flaw, guarantees both permanence and authenticity. Mlle de Scudéry has been seen as a distant harbinger of romanticism,[7] but the spirit of the *Carte de Tendre* is perhaps more obviously enshrined in the *sensibilité* which is characteristic of the early eighteenth century; there too, one finds the same awareness of problems of self-interest and deceit, and a revalorization of feeling as a solution to these problems. 'Ce ne sont pas les choses de dehors qui font la véritable satisfaction, ce sont les sentimens du coeur'; such a statement, made in 1660 (*Clélie*, VIII, 994), seems to anticipate literary history by at least fifty years. Mlle de Scudéry's view of *tendresse* as a derivative of *sensibilité* may be seen as an early manifestation of a change in social and literary attitudes which from the middle of the seventeenth century onwards sought increasingly to give primacy to feeling and to make reason an adjunct to it. The *Carte de Tendre* represents an ideal which is applicable both to *amitié* and to *amour*, an attempt to reinstate the affective dimension of life as the beginning and the end of all relationships. As such, the *Carte de Tendre* is more than a *carte d'amour*, although it contains insights into the nature of love, and still less is it a reduction of love to a frivolous pastime; it is rather a significant episode in the long battle for supremacy of the head and the heart.

NOTES AND REFERENCES

INTRODUCTION

1. Abbé Cotin, *Ménagerie* (n.p., n.d.), 7.

2. Ibid., 5f.

3. Tallemant des Réaux, *Historiettes*, edited by A. Adam, 2 vols (Paris 1960-61), II, 693.

4. Charles Sorel, *Les Discours pour et contre l'amitié tendre*, in *Oeuvres diverses* (Paris 1663), 174, 176.

5. Boileau, *Dialogue des héros de roman*, edited by T.F. Crane (Boston 1902), 192.

6. Boileau, *Oeuvres* (Paris 1961), 72.

7. Arnauld, *Lettre à M. P ... au sujet de la dixième Satire*, in Boileau, *Oeuvres*, 326-344 (*v* 335). Arnauld also claims that his view is shared by some well known personalities, notably the Princesse de Conti and Mme de Longueville.

8. Boileau, *Dialogue des héros de roman*, 192.

9. Arnauld, *Lettre ...*, 335.

10. Sorel, *Recueil des pièces en prose les plus agréables de ce temps*, 5 vols (Paris 1659-63), I, 87f.

11. Tallemant des Réaux, *Historiettes*, II, 690.

12. R. Lathuillère, *La Préciosité: étude historique et linguistique. Tome 1: Position du problème: les origines* (Geneva 1966), 102ff.

13. M. de Scudéry, *Artamène ou le Grand Cyrus*, 10 vols (Leyden and Paris, 1656), X, 351. Further references to *Le Grand Cyrus* are to this edition and are given after quotations in the text.

14. A. Niderst, *Madeleine de Scudéry, Paul Pellisson et leur monde* (Paris 1976), 236.

15. V. Cousin, *La Société française au XVIIe siècle d'après "Le Grand Cyrus" de Mlle de Scudéry*, 2 vols (Paris 1858), II, 151.

16. Sorel, *Les Discours pour et contre l'amitié tendre*, 189f.

17. E. Despois, 'Le Roman d'autrefois: Mademoiselle de Scudéry', *Revue des Deux Mondes* (1846), 455.

18. Dorothy Macdougall, *Madeleine de Scudéry, her romantic life and death* (London 1938), 73.

19. N. Aronson, *Mademoiselle de Scudéry* (Boston 1978), 42.

20. E. Magne, *Mme de la Suze et la société précieuse* (Paris 1908), 207.

21. P. Zumthor, 'La *Carte de Tendre* et les Précieux', *Trivium* VI (1948), 263-73 (*v* 270).

CHAPTER I

1. L. Belmont, 'Documents inédits sur la société et la littérature précieuses: extraits de la Chronique du Samedi publiés d'après le registre original de Pellisson (1652-7)', *Revue d'histoire littéraire de la France* IX (1902), 646-73.

2. E. Colombey, *Ruelles, salons et cabarets, histoire anecdotique de la littérature française* (Paris, 1858).

3. E. de Barthélémy, *Sapho, le Mage de Sidon, Zénocrate, étude sur la société précieuse d'après des lettre inédites de Mlle de Scudéry, de Godeau et d'Isarn* (Paris 1880).

4. Zumthor, 264f.

5. C. Aragonnès, *Madeleine de Scudéry, Reine du Tendre* (Paris, 1934), 158.

6. E. Magne, *Le Salon de Madeleine de Scudéry ou le royaume de Tendre* (Monaco, 1927), 21f.

7. G. Mongrédien, *Madeleine de Scudéry et son salon, d'après des documents inédits* (Paris, 1946), 72, 78.

8. Macdougall, 138.

9. Niderst, 125.

10. Sorel, *Dialogue de la prude et de la coquette*, in *Recueil des pièces en prose...*, IV, 109.

11. Barthélémy, 36.

12. The full text of the *Relation* is given by Barthélémy (op. cit., 43-9) and by Niderst (op. cit., 251ff.)

13. Niderst, 252.

14. Barthélémy, 43.

15. Niderst, 248, 253.

16. Colombey, 81.

17. For these various details, see Colombey, 63-73.

18. Ibid., 78-81.

19. The text of this decree is given in Barthélémy, 36ff, and in Mongrédien, 106ff.

20. Magne, *Le Salon de Madeleine de Scudéry ...*, 32.

21. *Discours Geografique, Pour l'vtilité de ceux qui veulent apprendre la carte pour aller de Particulier à Tendre*, in *Recueil Conrart* XI (Bibliothèque de l'Arsenal MS 5420), 435-40 (*v*. 440).

22. Ibid., 436, 438.

23. G. Boileau, *La Vie d'Epictete et l'Enchiridion ou L'Abbregé de sa Philosophie, avec le tableau de Cébès* (Paris, 1655), Preface, 229.

24. E.H. Wilkins, 'Vellutello's map of Vaucluse and the Carte de Tendre', *Modern Philology* XXIX (1931-2), 275-80.

25. Le Moyne, *Poésies* (Paris, 1650), 382; Mongrédien, 221.

26. Zumthor, 269.

27. Magne, *Le Salon de Madeleine de Scudéry ...*, 25f.

28. Zumthor, 269.

29. Somaize, *La Grande Description de l'Estat Incarnadin, nouuellement découuert par le Lieutenant General du Royaume de la Galanterie*, in *Recueil des pièces en prose ...*, IV, 137-233 (*v* 141).

30. *Recueil des pièces en prose ...*, II, 1-27 (*v* 25).

31. *Recueil des pièces en prose ...*, II, 259-62.

32. Zumthor, 265.

33. *Recueil des pièces en prose* ..., I, 324-31.

34. Abbé d'Aubignac. *Lettre d'Ariste à Cléonte, contenant l'Apologie de l'histoire du temps ou la Defense du royaume de Coqueterie* (Paris, 1659), 10, 8f.

35. Quotations from d'Aubignac's *Royaume de Coquetterie* are from the text given in *Voyages imaginaires, Songes, Visions, et Romans Cabalistiques*, edited by C. Garnier, 39 vols (Amsterdam, 1787-89), XXVI, 307-335.

CHAPTER II

1. Tallemant des Réaux, *Historiettes*, II, 690.

2. M. de Scudéry, *Clélie, histoire romaine*, 10 vols (Paris, 1655-61). Further references to *Clélie* are to this edition and are given after quotations in the text.

3. Niderst, 340f.

4. Ibid., 341.

5. The context suggests that when she speaks of 'générosité', Mlle de Scudéry is thinking of it as a principle which one knowingly chooses to live by, rather than as a spontaneous expression of the inner self; hence the rather slighting tone. On the other hand, in her letter to Mlle Dumoulin (cf. below, note 6), Mlle de Scudéry clearly sets store by *générosité*; in this case, presumably, it is not an adopted principle, but comes from the heart.

6. The text of the letters is given in Rathery and Boutron, *Mademoiselle de Scudéry, sa vie et sa correspondance* (Paris, 1873), 205.

7. Ibid., 400f.

8. Guéret, *Le Parnasse réformé*, 2e éd. (Paris, 1669), 117.

9. *Célinte, nouvelle première* (Paris, 1661), 194f.

10. Bougeant, *Voyage du Prince Fan-Férédin dans la Romancie*, in *Voyages imaginaires* ... XXVI, 1-156 (*v* 86f).

11. *Entretiens de Morale*, 2 vols (Paris, 1692), I, 44f.

CONCLUSION

1. M. de Scudéry, *Conversations morales*, 2 vols (Paris, 1686), II, 1014-5.

2. Zumthor, 271.

3. Ibid., 269. See also above, p. 33.

4. Saint François de Sales, *Traité de l'amour de Dieu*, 2 vols (Paris, 1934), I, 54.

5. Descartes, *Les Passions de l'âme*, in *Oeuvres*, edited by Adam and Tannery, 11 vols (Paris, 1964-74), XI, 388.

6. *La Théologie naturelle de Raymond Sebon*, translated by Montaigne (Paris, 1611), 248ff.

7. A. Adam, *Histoire de la littérature française au XVIIe siècle*, 5 vols (Paris, 1951), II, 139.